Strange Tales of the Civil War

By

Michael Sanders

BURD STREET PRESS
SHIPPENSBURG, PENNSYLVANIA

The acid-free paper used in this book meets the guidelines for permanence and durability of the Committee on Production Guidelines for Book Longevity of the Council on Library Resources.

For a complete list of available publications
please write
Burd Street Press
Division of White Mane Publishing Company, Inc.
P.O. Box 708
Shippensburg, PA 17257-0708 USA

Library of Congress Cataloging-in-Publication Data

Sanders, Michael, 1961-
    Strange tales of the Civil War / by Michael Sanders.
        p. cm.
    Includes bibliographical references and index.
    ISBN-13: 978-1-57249-271-4 ISBN-10: 1-57249-271-6 (acid-free paper)
    1. United States--History--Civil War, 1861-1865--Anecdotes. 2. Curiosities and wonders--Anecdotes. I. Title.

E655 .S26 2001
973.7--dc21
                                                                                2001037890

PRINTED IN THE UNITED STATES OF AMERICA

Contents

Contents

Illustrations

Acknowledgments

In the course of writing this book there have been many people who have helped obtain information, edit manuscripts, listen to ideas, and merely "put up" with the author's rambling about this story or that story.

In the foremost I would like to thank Sidney Dreese for his help in acquiring research materials and also his skills in photography; Michael Fohringer for lending an ear when I talked endlessly about the manuscript, as we explored various Civil War sites; Cindy Herman who edited the manuscript and provided a different perspective in the writing process; Bronwen Anderson who helped with the final proofing.

I would also like to thank the libraries and staffs of Penn State, Bucknell, and Susquehanna Universities. A special thank you goes to the United States Army Military History Institute at the Carlisle Barracks and their exceptional collection of resource material. In addition, Randy Hackenburg, at the USAMHI Photo Archives, deserves a great deal of credit for his assistance with obtaining many of the illustrations used in this book.

Introduction

Strange things happen in war. Men and women thrown into armed conflict seem to have a heightened sense of awareness. Emotions are high: fear, hate, anger, even happiness seem to be enhanced as they struggle through this period of time. Things once taken for granted become most precious. Feelings that were shrugged off become thoughts of foreboding. Dreams that used to be forgotten are analyzed. The sighting of an eagle or the appearance of a comet is sometimes interpreted as a sign of the future; possibly foretelling victory or disaster.

These emotions become even stronger during a civil war when a country is being torn apart at its very heart. Not only do people struggle to deal with the horror of war but also the horror of killing one's countrymen. The American Civil War was certainly no exception.

The characters in this book lived and fought through this great struggle in our nation's history. They told their dreams to friends and confided their fears to tent mates. They looked for signs of comfort and many times struggled to perform acts of courage that in their normal lives would be unthinkable. These tales are often overlooked but hold some merit as they were recorded many times by the very men that witnessed them. Their stories can be found in any number of newspapers, regimental histories and memoirs.

It is my hope that I have with this book of strange tales brought the Civil War to life and have given the reader a greater appreciation for that period of time in our nation's history.

Chapter One

Signs of the Times

Tearing the Union Apart

During the Civil War, as during so many struggles before and after, people have looked for signs of victory or defeat. Whether signs or omens, as many call them, really have a purpose is debatable. One person may view the appearance of a comet as a divine prophecy; while to another, it is just a meteorological phenomenon. No matter how one looks at such events, they still have the tendency to make us think and ponder their reason.

Julia Taft Bayne was a frequent visitor to the White House where she watched over her younger brother who was a close friend of Tad Lincoln. While visiting the Executive Mansion, she quickly became a favorite of the president and Mrs. Lincoln. However, Julia was not always responsible for her brother and did find herself involved with functions more to the liking of a teenage girl. On one occasion, Julia and her mother were invited to the White House for a flag-raising ceremony. In her book, *Tad Lincoln's Father*, Julia recalled the memorable event:

> There comes before my vision the brilliant group of generals and their aides, some members of the cabinet,

1

the cluster of ladies in hoopskirts and blossoming bonnets, and in the center the tall spare form of the President, so little known and valued then. When the moment came for the flag to be raised, the Marine Band began the national anthem and all arose, officers at salute, civilians uncovered. When the President pulled the cord, it stuck. He pulled harder, and suddenly the upper corner of the Union tore off and hung down. A gasp of surprise and horror at the sinister omen went around, but a young staff officer, with great presence of mind, stepped quickly to the group of ladies and extending his hand hissed imploringly, "Pins! Pins!"

They were supplied at once. Women had more pins in their clothes in those days. Mother took two out of her lace collar and some out of her dress. Mrs. Lincoln and the other ladies did the same, and the officer swiftly and efficiently pinned the corner and the flag was raised.

The band continued to play and the people on the grounds below, standing at attention, did not notice anything untoward except a slight delay in raising the flag. When we reached home and my father heard of the incident, he warned us not to mention the tearing of the stars out of the flag to any one.

"It will be suppressed," he said. "Some people are so superstitious. It might affect enlistments and we must have troops."[1]

Over the years, many flag-raising ceremonies have taken place without any problems. One must wonder why at that particular moment the flag tore. A total of nine stars were ripped from their field of blue. Even though eleven Southern states seceded from the Union, the tearing of nine was most certainly a shocking event to those who witnessed it. There is no record of Lincoln's thoughts during this incident. However, he too must have wondered about the significance of the national colors' being torn by his very hands.

Where Eagles Soar

One good omen that is mentioned many times in Civil War newsprint is the appearance of eagles—the symbol of the Federal republic. The April 24, 1861, *Lycoming Gazette* reported:

> While the big flag was being raised over Langdon & Diven's mill on Saturday, a large Eagle came and hovered for a few moments directly over the spot, and then departed due South. This incident is so well authenticated that there is no room for doubting its occurrence; and it is the more remarkable because an eagle is very rarely seen hereabouts. We have not seen one in fifteen years.[2]

Camp Curtin, a Union training facility located in Harrisburg, Pennsylvania, was also visited by an eagle during the spring of 1861. It was reported that

> . . . just as the men had seized the halyards, a large eagle, that came from no one knew where, hovered over the flag, and sailed majestically over the encampment, while the flag was run up. Thousands of eyes were upturned in a moment, and as the noble bird looked down, the cheers of three thousand men rent the air! Never was such ovation paid the "Imperial Bird of Jove." It lingered for a few moments, apparently not a particle

frightened at the terrific noise, then cleaving the air with its pinions, disappeared in the horizon.[3]

Yet another eagle sighting occurred as a Federal fleet made its way down the Chesapeake Bay to Hampton Roads, Virginia. As the ships weighed anchor and proceeded on their journey, a large bald eagle swept from the Maryland shore, soaring high above the fleet until finally coming to rest on the mast head of the USS *Atlantic*, which was serving as fleet headquarters. All eyes looked to the majestic bird and wondered about the nature of the visit. Was it a "blessing at parting, or some cunning secession rooster, intent on spying out the Federal strength?"[4] One rash soldier even had to be stopped from attempting to take a shot at the feathered visitor.

Although eagles have recently been reintroduced to the Keystone state, their sighting in Pennsylvania and even Maryland was, and still is, a rare occurrence. The sight of an eagle soaring the sky is inspiring. With its massive, outstretched wings, the bird of independence was extremely encouraging to those faithful to the flag and a sure sign that victory would be theirs.

The Union Shall Go On

By the end of 1863, the war began to look favorable for the Union. Victories at Gettysburg and Vicksburg helped to seal the fate of the Confederacy; but it would still take two more years of war to settle the issue. In Washington, life appeared almost normal. No longer were citizens seized with the fear of a Southern army marching down Pennsylvania Avenue. "Tourists came in droves, with money to spend. Northern capital had been invested in District enterprises and business in Washington was thriving as never before. . . . its residents, in the flush of a new prosperity, gazed on Washington with honest civic pride and felt a warm faith in the future of the city. The doubts of 1861 had vanished. . . ."[5]

Nowhere was this new feeling more obvious than at the Capitol building where the addition of the two congressional wings were under construction. This expansion project began in the early 1850s to meet the needs of a growing nation. Ironically, its chief proponent was a senator from Mississippi, Jefferson Davis.[6]

By 1863, the construction was nearly completed. New carpet had been laid in the Hall of Representatives. A massive bronze door depicting the life of Columbus was hung at the entrance of the corridor leading to the Old House Chamber. Painters were busy in the Senate wing while marble columns were placed into position on the portico.[7] As this work went on, the great dome grew steadily toward the heavens. It was an engineering marvel at the time, an inner and outer shell of cast iron metal weighing nine million pounds.[8]

Critics complained that the construction was unnecessary during a time of national emergency when the country's very existence was at stake. Lincoln, however, was committed to continuing the construction during the war and rebuffed the critics, stating, "if people see the Capitol going on it is a sign we intend the Union shall go on."[9]

With the dome nearing completion, the statue "Armed Liberty" was delivered to the Capitol grounds to await her ascent to the lantern structure on top of the dome. At $19\frac{1}{2}$ feet tall she was a classically robed woman. One hand leaned on a sword while the other rested on a shield, holding a wreath. Her head bore a helmet of an eagle head and feathers. Interestingly, sculptor Thomas Crawford originally designed a liberty cap fashioned after those worn by freed slaves in ancient Rome. However, due to objections from Jefferson Davis, who at the time was secretary of war and in charge of the Capitol project, the cap was changed to the eagle headdress.

The statue was assembled in five sections, with the head being placed atop the dome and bolted into place at noon on December 2, 1863. When the statue was completely assembled, a 35-gun salute was fired from the Capitol Hill Field Battery. One round was fired for each state, Northern as well as Southern. Another 35-gun salute was fired in return from the dozen forts that ringed the capital city. For the thousands of curious onlookers, the event had to be a reassuring sign of a bright and glorious future for the republic.[10]

Miss Taft also found herself present at the raising of the statue and recorded the event that stirred many to think peace may come at last:

> I was in the Capitol grounds with my father when the top of the great Statue of Liberty [Armed Liberty, not to be confused with the statue in New York Harbor] was swung into place by the big crane and carefully adjusted to its place. Just when the fastenings were pulled away a white dove, one of a flock which were always around the Capitol grounds, circled around the head of the statue and finally lighted there. It was seen by many people in the grounds and "a sign of peace" was in many mouths. My father said to me. "You must tell the president."[11]

It must have been a reassuring thought to Lincoln as he listened to the events of the day. Today "Armed Liberty" still

General Lee he mounted his horse and rode off. This was the last meeting between Lee and Jackson.

I have spoken of the falling of Jackson's sword because it strongly impressed me at the time as an omen of evil—an indefinable superstition such as sometimes affects persons on the falling of a picture or mirror. This feeling haunted me the whole day. . . .[12]

Late that afternoon Jackson placed his troops in position on the flank of the Union XI Corps. The attack came hard and swift as the Rebel yell echoed through the Wilderness. Soon the Union corps, stunned by the attack, was rolled up and fleeing back toward the Rappahannock River. Jackson rode forward with several members of his staff to personally scout the Union position.

While riding between the Union and Confederate lines, the scouting party was mistaken for Union cavalry and fired upon by Confederate infantry. Jackson was hit by three balls in the volley, one of which "penetrated the palm of his right hand. . . . A second passed around the wrist of the left arm and out through the left hand.

Lieutenant General Thomas "Stonewall" Jackson.
Courtesy MOLLUS-MASS at USAMHI

A third ball passed through the left arm half-way from shoulder to elbow. The large bone of the upper arm was splintered to the elbow-joint, and the wound bled freely."[13]

Jackson was sent by ambulance to a make-shift hospital set up near the Wilderness Tavern where surgery was begun. The first ball to be extracted was the one that had lodged in his hand. The surgeons then focused on the left arm and decided that amputation was the necessary course of action.[14] Sometime after the amputation the arm was taken outside. There it was buried with a complete religious ceremony. A marker still identifies the spot where the general's left arm resides.[15]

After the surgery, on Monday, May 14, Jackson was moved to the Chandler house where he could recover without the risk of capture by Union cavalry. For a time he appeared to be improving and even inquired how soon he could reenter active service. However, Thursday morning the general was found to be in great pain and suffering from pleuro-pneumonia of the right side. Dr. Hunter McGuire, Jackson's surgeon, felt this was caused by an incident on the night of his wounding, when one of the stretcher bearers was wounded in the arm and dropped the litter, causing Jackson to fall hard to the ground. Others have attributed this setback to a wet towel which Jackson placed on his stomach in an effort to relieve an attack of nausea he had early Thursday morning.

By Friday the pain in his right side disappeared, but his breathing was labored and the great general grew weaker. The next day the doctors informed his wife, Anna, who arrived the night before, that it was only a matter of time before the general would pass away. Jackson was still optimistic about his recovery but told his wife if he should die to bury him in Lexington, in the Valley of Virginia. On Sunday, May 10, his strength dwindled drastically. When told he was going to die that day he replied: "It is the Lord's Day; my wish is fulfilled. I have always desired to die on Sunday." Later that afternoon in his delirium he cried out, "Order A. P. Hill to prepare for action! Pass the infantry to the front rapidly! Tell Major Hawks . . . ," then the general stopped in midsentence. A smile spread over his pale face and quietly he spoke, "Let us cross over the river, and rest under the shade of the trees." The great Stonewall was dead.[16]

The Chandler house where Lieutenant General Thomas "Stonewall" Jackson died.

Chapter Two

Predictions

A Grave Flesh Wound

During late August 1862, the war in the eastern theater focused on Manassas Junction, Virginia, where Confederate General Thomas "Stonewall" Jackson raided a Union supply base. In response to this raid, Federal troops rushed to the area in an attempt to trap the elusive Jackson.

The 6th Wisconsin Infantry was among the Union regiments that rushed to Manassas Junction. After the column passed Gainesville, a small cluster of two or three houses, the men noticed a battery appearing from a wooded area, about a mile distant.[1] It wasn't known whether the guns were friend or foe. However, this question was soon answered when six shells screamed over the heads of the marching column. For many of the Federal troops, this was their first time under artillery fire. Captain Rufus Dawes of the 6th Wisconsin wrote, "surprise is no sufficient word for our astonishment."[2] The men were ordered to lie down next to the road bank for protection, while the fence bordering the pike was torn down to allow the 4th U.S. Artillery to gallop into position. The 2nd Wisconsin was ordered to assault the Rebel guns. The Wisconsin men formed their battleline and advanced. As the

General Thomas "Stonewall" Jackson's Confederate troops
raid Union supplies at Manassas Junction.

Courtesy *Battles and Leaders of the Civil War*

Federals crested an intervening hill, they were opened upon
by a heavy volley of musketry on the right flank. The Wisconsin men replied in kind and the battle was opened. It was
quickly ascertained that more men were needed on the firing
line, and the remainder of the brigade was quickly ordered
up to support the 2nd. The 6th Wisconsin immediately responded to the word "march" and scrambled up the embank-
ment and over the fence. This was their first real fight and
they were going headlong into the storm.[3]

In the ranks of the 6th Wisconsin, Company E, stood
Private Major (name not rank) Garfield who nervously
awaited his first battle. Garfield had a sickening feeling in his
stomach, and the fear of death surrounded him. Several weeks

prior in Fredericksburg, Garfield had informed a close friend
of his prediction that "he would be wounded in the first battle
he went into and die from the effects of it."[4]

The line moved forward into the fight, as did Garfield
and the rest of the 6th Wisconsin. The battle raged on with
heavy casualties on both sides, until darkness finally halted
hostilities. Across the fields, wounded soldiers forced their
bleeding bodies toward the rear of the battlelines. Major
Garfield limped among them. He had been struck in the leg
by a minie ball. After being hit, he called out to his comrades, "I'm hit; good-bye boys."[5] His prediction had come
true—he had been shot in his first battle—but certainly a leg
wound was not life-threatening. The young man slowly made
his way to the rear in search of a surgeon. Finding the aid
station, Garfield showed his leg to a surgeon. The doctor examined the wound and informed Garfield that "yours is a
flesh wound in the calf, and in a few days you will be all
right."[6] Garfield's response to the doctor was, "tell my par-
ents I did not shirk my duty."[7] With those words he lay down
without complaint and died.

"Faithful Unto Death"

During December 1862, the Union Army of the
Potomac set out on another campaign to capture the Confederate capital, Richmond. This new plan involved crossing
the Rappahannock River at Fredericksburg, Virginia, and pro-
ceeding overland to the capital city. In the path of the Union
force stood the Confederate Army of Northern Virginia, commanded by General Robert E. Lee. The Southern commander
had carefully positioned his army on heights in back of the
town. All day on December 12, the Union army positioned

itself for the next day's attack. That night was a restless one for men on both sides of the war. The troops of the 6th Pennsylvania Infantry were no exception to the rule, and for Sergeant Frank Bailey the night was exceptionally sleepless.

It was the night before the battle that six of us, all of Company H, stretched our weary limbs under the warm cover of an A tent to get rest and strength for the struggle on the morrow. . . .

Our suppers had been finished, pipes smoked, tents pitched, and we prepared for our last sleep before the battle. . . . Lieutenant [Reuben] Pratt, recently married to a young and lovely girl, had returned from a furlough home only a few weeks before. . . . About midnight I felt a pull at my elbow, and rousing up saw Lieutenant Pratt bending over me, motioning for me to come out of the tent without disturbing our sleeping comrades. We had been warm friends and next door neighbors for years before entering the army, and I thought I had for some days detected a shade of sadness in his countenance, and more than once had found him engrossed in melancholy thought, but I had attributed it to the fact that his mind was on his wife and friends he had so recently left behind him. We walked out to the dying embers of the fire and sat down for some moments without speaking; he probably thinking whether or not it would be better to tell what was on his mind, and I waiting to hear.

At last, with a deep feeling, he said:

"F_____ [Frank], I have a premonition of death. Six weeks ago, while on my way from home, I stopped in Washington over Sunday, and on Sunday evening attended church. When I crossed the threshold of the church the gas lights dimmed, and then recovered their usual brightness. The presentiment came to me in a moment, that I should be killed in the next battle, and I have not been able to overcome it since. I feel as certain, as that you and I are here, that I shall be killed tomorrow."

I tried with the best argument I could to dissuade him from the idea, and to show him the fallacy of tracing any connection between a thing which he had so often seen and was of such common occurrence in his own life. But argument was useless, and he seemed as sure of his death as though it were a positive certainty. I knew that he was morally and physically a brave man, and his deeply religious soul would have rebelled against anything like superstition, so that his feelings could not be attributed to cowardice, or a desire to shirk the dangers before us; besides, he had been tried on hard-fought fields, and proved true as steel. With him the idea was a wrought conviction admitting no doubt, and I pitied him from the bottom of my heart; though not a believer in presentiments, I could not feel with him that his death was a foregone conclusion. After an hour's conversation on the subject we again retired; he to a sleepless preparation for the death of which he felt so sure, I to indulge in selfish slumber.

With the first breath of dawn we were aroused to eat a hearty breakfast and fall into line. A dense fog covered the whole plain, and we moved cautiously forward, unable to see more than a few yards. Soon a skirmish line encountered the rebel pickets, who promptly fell back after a few shots. A halt was called, and our division, the old Pennsylvania Reserves, received orders to unsling knapsacks, and we knew we had been selected to make the charge on the left. Moving forward we were placed in close column by brigades, in support of a battery, and ordered to lie down. The rising sun soon cleared away the fog and revealed our line of battle face to face with the enemy who were concealed in the woods about 600 yards distant. Then the dogs of war were let loose, and the several batteries along our line began to pay their respects to the enemy, who answered the compliment with vigor. Then the solid shot from the enemy's right raked our lines from left to right, while spherical case, screeching through the clear morning air from the front, exploded over our heads. . . . Through all this trying ordeal Pratt kept his self-possession and strove only to do his duty, though no one but myself knew the deep and silent agony he was struggling to conceal.

At last, to our relief, we were ordered to fix bayonets and charge. Never did the gallant 6th keep a straighter line on a dress parade than it did while charging across the 600 yards of open field which lay between us and the enemy. The railroad which ran along the skirt of the woods was the point at which we were to stop, but finding the position untenable by reason of a battery which swept the track, we entered the woods and kept after the enemy, whose first line was broken and now in full retreat, mowing a track the width of the division through the rebel lines. A lull occurring in the firing, Pratt again approached me, and leading the way a few paces to the rear, said with a voice choking with emotion:

"I shall never leave these woods alive. I am going to meet death here this afternoon. If you get out alive, I want you to tell Jennie I was prepared for death, and that my last thoughts were of duty to her, my country, and my God."

I was deeply impressed with his earnestness, and begged him to go to the rear out of danger, but of no avail. He felt he was going to die, and he would meet a soldier's death as a soldier should.

"Forward," came the order along the line, and with a hasty "Good-bye" and "God bless you," we sprang to our places to encounter the rapidly forming lines of our enemy's fresh reinforcements.

That was the last time I ever saw Pratt. The straggling shots deepened into that loud, monotonous roll, and the stray whiz of the minie ball changed into that storm of leaden hail when sounds lose their individuality, denoting the desperate nature of battle. A sharp twinge in my shoulder gave me a ticket to the rear, and I left the boys still pressing forward. . . . Night mercifully put an end to the slaughter, and the lines were reformed near where we started in the morning.

With great anxiety I sought out our company, with several others who had been wounded to learn how it had fared with the rest of the boys. Out of the six who had slept together the night before, five went into battle, two of whom were killed, and two wounded. Almost the last man killed was poor Pratt, struck in the forehead with a minie ball. He never spoke afterwards, and the boys being hard pressed, were reluctantly compelled to leave his body where he fell. His presentiment was no idle tale. His prediction proved as true as he felt it to be, and was carried out in all its terrible reality. With the flickering gas in the church at Washington the light of his life went out in the fullness of the undying fame due to the dead heroes of the war for the Union. Among the serried hosts of immortal spirits which are gathering in silent array on the battlements of heaven, he rests with the coveted crown inscribed "Faithful unto death."[8]

Private Scott's Anguish

During the beginning of May 1863 the Battle of Chancellorsville raged in an area called the Wilderness. On May 1, the 125th Pennsylvania moved into position on the Plank Road nearly a half mile from the Chancellor Mansion. The regiment began building fortifications along both sides of the road. Colonel Jacob Higgins wrote in his official report that the men used "fortifications of brush, saplings, underwood, and dirt, using our hatchets and knives instead of axes, bayonets and pointed sticks for picks, and tin plates and hands as substitutes for shovels."[9] Diligently, the 125th raised a double row of defenses to allow one line of troops to lie on the road while a second line occupied the road's berm.

At one point during the day Private John W. Scott of Company I became anxious about his chances of surviving the battle and approached Captain William Wallace of Company C. Private Scott handed the captain his watch, saying, "here is a watch I want to leave with you to send to my mother."[10] Wallace, reluctant to help the distressed private, replied that he himself had a better risk of being killed in the forthcoming battle and advised Scott to see one of the sutlers about the matter.

Private Scott and the rest of the 125th Pennsylvania were no strangers to battle. They were mustered into service on August 13, 1862, as a nine-month regiment and were initiated into warfare one month later at Antietam. During the battle, they participated in the desperate fighting at the Dunkard Church where they received many casualties.[11]

The 125th held their position on the Plank Road, occasionally venturing forth to rout Rebel troops in their front.[12] But by Sunday morning, May 3, Confederate forces were able to move closer to the Chancellor Mansion after a successful attack the evening before, led by Major General Thomas "Stonewall" Jackson. The next morning the 125th came under intense fire from Confederate artillery that had moved into position during the previous night. The barrage quickly made the position untenable for the 125th, forcing them to abandon the position north of the Chancellor Mansion. During the day the 125th suffered minimal casualties even though they were under terrible fire from Rebel guns. In Company I the only man killed was Private John Scott. Sadly just 15 days later, the nine-month term of enlistment expired and the men of the 125th were mustered out of the service.[13]

Mustered Out

During the siege of Richmond and Petersburg, which lasted from June 1864 through April 1865, the Union army attempted to cut Southern supply lines into the city. By cutting these lines, the Confederate Army of Northern Virginia would eventually have to surrender or evacuate the city. One such attempt was the attack on the Weldon Railroad,

Union artillery placed across the Plank Road near the
Chancellor Mansion during the Battle of Chancellorsville.

Courtesy *Battles and Leaders of the Civil War*

which connected Petersburg with Weldon, North Carolina.
The movement was made on August 18, 1864, by the Union V
Corps commanded by Major General Gouverneur K. Warren.[14]

Second Lieutenant John Timmons of the 6th Wisconsin
Volunteers viewed the movement against the Weldon Railroad
as an unwelcome mission. He was due to be mustered out on
July 15, 1864, but his orders were late in arriving.[15] During
the march he turned to a friend and spoke of his fear and
regret at not going home. "This is tough," he said. "I ought
to have been mustered out and gone home a month ago. In a
day or two we shall have a fight and I shall go to my long
home—be killed."[16]

Later that day, the assault on the Weldon Railroad began as Union troops pulled up the tracks and bent the rails
so they could not be used again. During this time, the 6th
Wisconsin was relieved of any heavy action and served only
as skirmishers, to the delight of Lieutenant Timmons.

The next day, the 6th Wisconsin, along with the rest of the brigade, was ordered to fill a hole in the Union line, connecting the V Corps with the Union entrenchments in front of Petersburg. The 6th once again drew a fortunate lot, being placed in the rear as a reserve. Suddenly, at about four o'clock in the afternoon, a Rebel division burst out of the thickets.[17] From both the right and rear Rebel troops poured a deadly fire into the thin Union brigade line. Another assault erupted to the front.[18] Regiment after regiment was overrun by the fury of the combined Confederate assaults. The 6th Wisconsin moved forward in an attempt to stop the gray tide, but soon collapsed from the Rebel pressure and joined the rest of the retreating brigade.[19] Timmons struggled to make it to the rear but fate intervened. Sergeant James Sullivan, who was running behind Timmons, witnessed the scene: "One shot struck an officer [Timmons] who was in front of me, in the back of the head and it seemed to me it knocked the whole top of his head off."[20] John Timmons never did make it back to his home in Wisconsin, instead his prediction was realized near the Weldon Railroad on that day in August 1864.

Death at Winchester

By the summer of 1864 control of the Shenandoah Valley became a great concern of the Union high command. This region of Western Virginia had supplied a great deal of foodstuffs to the Confederate war effort, and was also used as a highway for Southern armies to march into Northern territory. To alleviate the concern over the valley's control, Major General Philip Sheridan was appointed to command the newly organized Army of the Shenandoah Valley.

Sheridan immediately began working to clear the valley of any Confederate troops. On September 19, he ordered an attack on the Confederate II Corps, which was encamped outside Winchester, Virginia. Lieutenant Colonel Aaron W. Ebright of the 126th Ohio Volunteers was among those under Sheridan's command. Ebright was apprehensive before the attack. He confessed to Colonel J. Warren Keifer, Second Brigade commander in the Second Division of the VI Corps, a premonition of his death and that he would not live to see the battle finished. Ebright then asked Keifer to write to his wife and send his remains and effects home to Lancaster, Ohio.[21]

All day the battle-lines wavered back and forth. Late in the afternoon the 126th Ohio was ordered to push forward to dislodge Rebel defenders around the Dinkle Farm buildings near the center of the Confederate line. Lieutenant Colonel Ebright, who had survived several charges during the day, once again led his men forward in the final assault of the day.[22] While urging his men on from horseback, a Confederate ball found its mark and pierced Ebright's breast. Lieutenant Colonel Aaron W. Ebright fell from his horse

Lieutenant Colonel Aaron W. Ebright, killed September 19, 1864, at Winchester, Virginia.

Courtesy Scott Hilts Collection at USAMHI

and died instantly, bringing his premonition of death from earlier that same day to fruition.[23]

A President Gets His Head Examined

During the late 18th and early 19th century the pseudo-science of phrenology developed. Practitioners of phrenology examined the size and contours of a person's head to determine individual characteristics and intelligence levels. It was based on the theory that "every element of taste and aversion, of hope and fear, of love and hatred, as well as intellectual faculties and memory, have their special seats in some part of the brain."[24]

Phrenology originated with German physician Franz Joseph Gall. During his time in medical school he observed that his classmates with the best memories also had prominent eyes. Gall theorized that an organ of visual memory was placed behind the eyes.[25] This theory was eventually expanded to include a total of 37 organs or regions of the brain.[26] Each organ, it was thought, was responsible for a different part of a person's character. For example, it was believed that the organs of intellect were situated in the forehead, or anterior lobes of the brain. Characteristics of social nature were believed to be located in the back of the head, or the posterior portion of the brain.[27]

Phrenology appealed to all social classes. Many famous personalities of the era such as President James Garfield, poet Walt Whitman, abolitionist John Brown, Mormon Church founder Joseph Smith, and famous Siamese twins Chang and Eng, had their heads examined and the results made public. Others like Clara Barton, founder of the American Red Cross, entered her first job as a school teacher on the advice of a phrenologist. Even royalty gave in to the allure of having a cranial exam; Queen Victoria and Prince Albert had their children's heads examined.[28]

These examinations were not just performed on famous individuals in the cities; practitioners also traveled throughout the country and examined the heads of average citizens. One such examination took place in Point Pleasant, Ohio. Like many small towns in the United States in 1832, any show was welcome to provide entertainment. When a distinguished phrenologist arrived in Point Pleasant to set up shop for a few days, the 180 inhabitants became quite excited.[29]

During one show, a young boy sat down in the chair for his reading. The examiner first looked over the shape of the youth's head. He then began a series of measurements and wrote each down on a chart. Next, the practitioner gently felt the head to further determine its shape and contour. The examiner soon finished his lengthy study and offered a prediction that astonished the boy and the crowd: "You need not be surprised if you see this boy fill the presidential chair some time."[30]

Of course, such a prognosis was risky. After all, what was the chance of a boy from a town of only 180 inhabitants becoming president? The

Ulysses S. Grant, 18th president of the United States.

Courtesy MOLLUS-MASS at USAMHI

boy did graduate from the West Point Military Academy and served in the War with Mexico. He eventually resigned from the army under difficult circumstances, and although he was 40 years old when the Civil War broke out, he decided to renew his military career. Within one year he became a leading general and national hero. Certainly most everyone had forgotten about the prediction the phrenologist had made many years earlier. Even the little boy who grew up to be a national hero and president quite possibly never imagined his destiny, yet it was fulfilled when Ulysses S. Grant became the 18th president of the United States.

Straggling unto Death

In June 1863, General Robert E. Lee led the Army of Northern Virginia north to invade Pennsylvania. Following him was the Union Army of the Potomac under its newly appointed commander, Major General George Meade. The Union army was forced to march rapidly in pursuit of its counterpart, covering many miles during hot and humid days. Even though the march was long, for some men the journey would not prove long enough—these were the roads that would lead to their deaths. Private James Perkins was one of these men. He was a member of the 37th Massachusetts, in the Third Division of Major General John Sedgwick's VI Corps.

After the Battle of Chancellorsville, Perkins had a premonition that he would be killed in the 37th's next engagement. His comrades tried to talk him out of the foolish idea, but to no avail. Even his bunk mate, Private Charles Babbitt, tried to argue him out of the idea, but Perkins persisted that his life was doomed.[31]

On June 6, the VI Corps, including the 37th Massachusetts, left its base around Fredericksburg, Virginia, and began marching northward. It was the last of the seven corps of the Union army to move.[32] By June 17, the regiment made its bivouac at Fairfax Station, and pitched their tents on the Chantilly battlefield the following evening. The 37th remained at Fairfax Courthouse for the following six days until they were ordered to move north another six miles to Centreville, near the Bull Run battlefield. The next day Dranesville was reached, the day after Edwards Ferry, then the 37th crossed the Potomac River and found itself once again in Union territory. During June 28, the regiment passed Poolesville, Barnesville, and Hyattstown until 28 miles were finally completed by midnight. June 30 found the 37th Massachusetts retiring into the fields around Manchester, Maryland, with another 20 miles completed. The last five days were grueling for the men of the 37th Massachusetts, as they had marched an average of 25 miles each day in rain and intense heat.

During the afternoon of July 1, while encamped at Manchester, the sound of cannons could be heard to the northwest. Word soon came that contact was made between the two armies at the crossroads town of Gettysburg, Pennsylvania. That night and the next day the 37th Massachusetts moved north on the Baltimore Pike in a forced march to Gettysburg.[33]

Along the route anything that became a burden to carry in the heat and humidity of the day was pitched to the side of the road. Not only did blankets and other accouterments litter the wayside, but stragglers also lingered there; too tired to go on, they turned out of the ranks to be left behind. Some sat nursing sore, callous feet, while others slept. During the 30-mile march, the 37th Massachusetts suffered its share of stragglers. One of these was Private James Perkins.[34]

At about 5 P.M. on July 2 the 37th Massachusetts arrived with the rest of the VI Corps on the fields outside Gettysburg. The second day's battle was in full force as Confederate Lieutenant General James Longstreet's Corps attacked the left of the Union line. Immediately, the VI Corps was placed in support of the V Corps, commanded by Major General George Sykes, who was defending Little Round Top. The 37th was badly worn from the exhausting march and fortunately was spared from going into the battle that day.[35]

As the third day of the great battle began, the Massachusetts men listened to the fighting on the right of the Union line at Culp's Hill. They remained in reserve and had not yet actively participated in the battle. Soon orders for the Second Brigade were received to reinforce the Union line on Culp's Hill. The 37th, along with the other regiments in the brigade, anticipated action and marched behind the Union line toward the sound of the fighting. However, as they neared the hill, word came that the Confederates had withdrawn their attack and reinforcements were not needed.

With the urgency of the moment gone, the men were allowed to rest before returning to their former position. During this rest period Perkins finally caught up with the regiment. It was good timing as the fields around Gettysburg were relatively quiet. Nearby, troops were enjoying the peace by eating a quick meal. Others were reading and still others caught up on some much-needed sleep. Even the Union high command enjoyed a break in the action as Major Generals George Meade, Winfield Scott Hancock, and several other corps commanders enjoyed a stewed chicken for lunch. The time was one o'clock.[36]

The halt was soon over and the men of the 37th Massachusetts picked themselves up from their rest to begin the march back to their former position. Filing out of the grove, the Massachusetts men soon came to the Taneytown Road. James Bowen recorded what happened next in his *History of the Thirty-Seventh Massachusetts*:

> Suddenly, with no more warning than a preliminary shell or two that went far overhead as to scarcely attract an upward glance of the eye, a murderous fire burst from the distant batteries, striking the regiment in the flank with wonderful precision and doing frightful execution. . . . Shells burst in the faces of the men, tore terrible, bleeding gaps through the ranks, crashed in resonant fury against the stone-wall and rocks bordering the road, rent the old board fence at the left into hurtling fragments. . .[37]

"Steady, Thirty-seventh! Forward, double quick!"[38] shouted Colonel Oliver Edwards, commander of the 37th Massachusetts, as the troops moved through the hail of steel coming from the Confederate guns. As the regiment moved forward, Perkins turned to his friend Charles Babbitt and said, "Charley, this is pretty tough, to nearly march your life out to get here to be killed."[39]

During the next few moments, Perkins' words of his fate became evident as Babbitt wrote, "The words were scarcely spoken when a piece of shell struck him over the right ear and passed through his head, coming out above the left eye, killing him instantly. I fell over his body as he was breathing his last."[40] James Perkins' presentiment of death had come true on the bloody fields of Gettysburg.

Meeting Fate in the Wilderness

In the spring of 1864, the Union army emerged from its winter in Culpeper, Virginia, to begin the war anew. The wet, cold weather finally turned warm and the roads became passable for its large contingent and machinery. The goal was to capture the Confederate capital, Richmond, and do as much damage to the Confederate Army of Northern Virginia as possible.

On May 4, the 6th Wisconsin was ordered to march to the Germanna Ford on the Rapidan River. At this point, the men crossed into the Wilderness, a dense tangle of trees and bushes in Northern Virginia. The day was relatively quiet and they found themselves bivouacked for the night at the Old Wilderness Tavern.[41] Major Philip Plummer of the 6th Wisconsin Infantry knew very well that the next day would bring new fighting and more dying. He had been depressed all day during the march, and even his fellow officers noticed and teased him about the change in his attitude. Plummer coarsely replied to his colleagues, "Have all the fun with me you desire, gentlemen; it is your last chance."[42]

The next day, May 5, the march resumed through the tangled trees and brush. The 6th made contact with lead elements of the Confederate army and was ordered into battle formation, being placed on the left side of the second line. As Captain John A. Kellogg began to fall into the battleline, Major Plummer inquired of him: "What word shall I send to your wife?"

"Never mind my wife," replied Kellogg, "look after Converse's girl!"

To this remark Captain Rollin Converse replied, "Plummer will be shot before either of us, leave your messages with Dawes, he is the only man they can't kill!"[43]

At noon the line started forward; the men moved cautiously, aware that at any time the surrounding woods could explode with a hail of minie balls.[44] The 7th Indiana led the assault at about one hundred paces. Major Plummer and the other officers of the 6th tried to keep the colors of the Indiana regiment within sight to support the lead regiment. The assaulting column advanced about one mile, when suddenly the Indiana troops were ordered to move at the double-quick. The men of the 6th hurried as fast as they could to keep up through the thick tangle of brush. A burst of musketry echoed through the trees as the Union line reached within 40 paces of waiting Rebels hidden by the thick underbrush. The Federals immediately returned fire, throwing the Confederate line into confusion. The Indiana men charged the stunned Rebels with bayonets, driving them backward into a second line. The Southern battle line was routed, leaving their dead and dying on the field. In the confusion of the assault and tangle of brush, Federal troops on the left stopped their assault, stranding the men of the 6th and the rest of the brigade.[45]

The retreating Confederates soon received reinforcements, and launched a counterattack on the lone Federal brigade.[46] The shrill echo of the Rebel yell rose up through the trees. Glancing to his right, Major Plummer was stunned at the sight and immediately shouted to Lieutenant Colonel Rufus Dawes to "look to the right."[47]

Dawes reported that "There came the enemy stretching as far as I could see through the woods, and rapidly advancing and firing upon us. I ordered a change of front on the color company, to bring the regiment to face them. Directing Major Plummer to attend to the left wing, I gave the orders to the right wing, but the Major was shot and killed."[48] The Rebel reinforcements were able to flank the Union line. The Federal battleline quickly reeled, falling back to its original position of earlier in the day.[49]

The 6th Wisconsin lost forty or fifty men during the day. Major Plummer's body was found, rolled into a blanket and buried near the area where he gave his life for the Union. Never again did his fellow officers have fun with Major Plummer.[50]

Chapter Three

Coincidences

Lexington, Concord, and Baltimore

When Lincoln asked for 75,000 volunteers on April 15, 1861, to suppress the rebellion, patriotic men, by the thousands, lined up to make their mark on muster sheets for the defense of the nation. At this time the defenses of Washington, D.C. were hardly adequate and the city became a prime target for an early Rebel strike. Pennsylvania immediately sent five companies of men to protect the capital. These five companies from the Keystone state would thereafter be named "the first defenders."[1]

Massachusetts quickly followed in kind with the 6th Massachusetts Volunteers. The credit for the quick response of the Massachusetts men belongs to Colonel Edward Jones, commander of the 6th Massachusetts. Volunteers from Middlesex and Essex Counties reported for duty on April 16, 1861. Having filled their ranks before any other regiment in the state, the 6th was given the honor of being the first Massachusetts regiment to depart for Washington.[2] Only two days after Lincoln's call for help, the men of the 6th were drawn up in front of the Massachusetts State House in Boston. The men stood proud and erect as they received their colors and a

farewell from Massachusetts Governor John Andrew.[3] Soon
after the ceremony the men of the 6th boarded a train bound
for Washington. However, before arriving in the capital city,
the 6th had to pass through Baltimore, a hotbed of the Seces-
sionist movement.

Three days later, on April 19 at 10 A.M., the train pulled
into the President Street Depot, Baltimore. The streets were
fairly quiet, as the early arrival of the train took any potential
troublemakers by surprise.[4] Horses had to be hitched to the
cars to ferry them to the Camden Street Depot across the
city.[5] At first the transfer went well, as only slight demonstra-
tions were made. However, word soon spread throughout the
city that the Massachusetts Regiment had arrived.

By the time the seventh car started across the city, the
crowd had grown in size and temper. Before long this car
came under a hail of bricks and paving stones as it slowly
made its way through the mob. Inside, the Massachusetts
men grew anxious for their safety. The men were forbidden
to shoot into the crowd unless fired upon. As the mob grew
angrier, gunshots were fired. In response, officers allowed the
militia men to respond to the threat. Finally the seventh car
arrived at the Camden Street Depot.[6]

Since the mob failed to stop the first cars, they turned
their attention to the remaining ones, which contained Companies C, D, I, and L.[7] To slow the progress of these cars the
mob placed heavy ship anchors on the tracks that were near
the wharf, while others simply busied themselves tearing up
the rails.[8]

Captain Albert Follansbee of the Lowell Company ordered the men to file out of the cars and prepare to march the
one mile to the depot. Almost immediately the mob pelted

the company with bricks. Captain Follansbee relates what happened next:

> As soon as the order was given, the brickbats began to fly into our ranks from the mob. I called a policeman, and requested him to lead the way to the other depot. He did so. After we had marched about a hundred yards we came to a bridge. The Rebels had torn up most of the planks. We had to play 'Scotch hop' to get over it. As soon as we crossed the bridge they commenced to fire upon us from the streets and houses. We were loaded, but not capped. I ordered the men to cap their rifles and protect themselves; and then we returned their fire, and laid a great many of them away. I saw four fall on the sidewalk at one time. They followed us up, and we fought our way to the other depot—about one mile. They kept at us until the cars started. Quite a number of the rascals were shot after we entered the cars. [9]

During the day the 6th Massachusetts received its first taste of war and death. In its ranks a total of four were killed while fighting with the mob. They included Corporal Summer Needham of Company I, along with Privates Addison Whitney, Luther Ladd, and Charles Taylor from Company D.[10] Ironically these men were all from Middlesex County, Massachusetts. In a twist of fate, 86 years earlier on April 19, 1775, men from Middlesex County, Massachusetts, had been the first to die during Battles of Lexington and Concord.

Lived Together, Died Together

Franklin Gerlaugh and William Black were best friends who shared almost every experience in life including the same birthday. When news of war reached their hometown of Freedom, Wisconsin, the two boys could not resist the urge to sign up and fight for the Union.[11]

They soon found themselves in a throng of activity at Camp Randall, located just outside Madison, the capital of Wisconsin. At the camp, Gerlaugh and Black became tent mates and trained for war. They were assigned to the 6th Wisconsin Volunteer Infantry along with 1,043 other men from across the Badger state.[12]

On September 17, 1862, the 6th Wisconsin and the rest of the Army of the Potomac were encamped on the north side of Antietam Creek, near the town of Sharpsburg, Maryland. Directly to the south, the Army of Northern Virginia waited for the inevitable collision. During the early morning hours the conflict opened with a Union attack on the left of the Confederate line. The 6th Wisconsin formed part of the assaulting column. With colors waving in the morning Maryland air, the men of the 6th moved forward toward the Dunkard Church, a plain white one-room building that would soon be the focal point of some of the most horrific fighting of the war. Almost immediately, a shell whistled over their heads. Rebel cannoneers had found their target in the midst of the charging column. "So accurate was his range," reported Colonel Edward Bragg of the 6th Wisconsin, "that the second shell exploded in the ranks, disabling 13 men."[13]

As the regiment neared the cornfield, the right of the line was forced onto the Hagerstown Pike, which ran straight past the Dunkard Church and into Sharpsburg. Confederate artillery was now joined with small arms fire that blazed forth from a wooded area known as the West Woods. In addition, more Rebel fire erupted in the front, forcing the Wisconsin men to seek shelter in the cornfield. The men who had been caught on the Hagerstown Pike fell to the ground to avoid the deadly missiles.[14]

In the midst of the carnage, Franklin Gerlaugh was shot in the head. His body violently reeled backward as his life-long friend, William Black, turned to look on in horror. Before Black had a chance to respond, he also received a fatal wound in the throat.[15] The two best friends, who had come into the world on the same day, exited within seconds of each other as they lay side by side in a cornfield hundreds of miles from home.

Gerlaugh and Black were buried in the same grave at Keedysville, Maryland. Their epitaph reads: "To the Memory

William Black and Franklin Gerlaugh lie at rest side by side in the Antietam National Cemetery.

Courtesy Sidney Dreese

of Franklin Gerlaugh and William P. Black, aged respectively nineteen years, five months and twenty-one days. Killed at the battle of Antietam, Sept. 17, 1862. Rest, Soldier."[16] Sometime after the war, the two friends were removed from Keedysville and placed in the Antietam National Cemetery where they lie beside other Union men who died that same day in the same cornfield in Maryland.

In the Beginning and in the End

In July 1861, as war was drawing ever so close, the Federal army that had gathered in Washington was preparing to march on Richmond by an overland route through Manassas Junction. Standing in the way of this advance was the Confederate Army of the Potomac commanded by General Pierre Gustave Toutant Beauregard.

General Beauregard made his headquarters in the house of farmer Wilmer McLean. Because roads near the property led directly to Manassas Junction, it was thought that the Union army might attempt to force the passage on the nearby fords. For this reason the McLean farm was a natural position for the Southern headquarters.

On July 21, the much anticipated Battle of Bull Run was finally fought on the ground west of the McLean farm. The McLean farm was spared of any destruction by the First Battle of Bull Run. But Wilmer McLean had seen enough of war. His fields had been trampled. His house had been invaded by Beauregard and his staff. Wilmer McLean wanted nothing more to do with the war and had only one thing left that he could do—move his family to a place the war would never touch.

* * * * *

Four years later McLean and his family lived in the small village of Appomattox Courthouse, Virginia. Battles raged over the tidewater region to the east and in the Shenandoah Valley to the west, but for McLean the war was far away. In April 1865, the peace McLean had found was abruptly shattered. The trenches defending Richmond and Petersburg were abandoned by the Confederate Army of Northern Virginia in an effort to escape the overwhelming numbers of Federal troops. As the Southern troops retreated, they were constantly shadowed and molested by Union horsemen on their flank, while the massive Federal infantry followed behind waiting to deal a fatal blow.

The Wilmer McLean house near Manassas Junction served as General Beauregard's headquarters during the First Battle of Bull Run.

Lee sent a letter to Grant informing the Union commander of his intention to seek terms for the surrender of the Army of Northern Virginia. In reply, Grant asked Lee to set up a place where the two generals could discuss terms. The task to locate a suitable location fell upon Lee's aide-de-camp, Colonel Charles Marshall. Marshall recalls in his memoirs, "General Lee told me to go forward and find a house where he could meet General Grant, and of all people, whom should I meet but McLean. . . . He took me into a house that was all dilapidated and that had no furniture in it. I told him it wouldn't do. Then he said, 'Maybe my house will do!'"[17]

Finding the residence suitable, Marshall summoned Lee to the house to await Grant's arrival. With the arrival of Grant the two men exchanged courtesies and then proceeded to the business at hand. Grant explained the terms, which were generous. Officers and men surrendered would be paroled and disqualified from taking up arms again until properly exchanged. All arms, ammunition, and supplies were to be considered captured property. In addition side arms of officers, their private horses, and baggage were to be retained by them. Following a brief discussion, Lee suggested that cavalry and artillery horses were the private property of individual soldiers. Grant consented, stating that the horses would be needed by these men to work their farms during the spring planting. The terms were thus agreed upon.[18]

With the meeting over, another drama unfolded that stunned Wilmer McLean. His furniture had become valuable historical artifacts. Major General Philip Sheridan handed him 20 dollars in gold. In the general's hands was the small oval table on which Lee had signed the letter agreeing to the surrender terms. Turning to Brevet Major General George

The Wilmer McLean house at Appomattox was the site where Confederate General Robert E. Lee surrendered the Army of Northern Virginia to Lieutenant General Ulysses S. Grant on April 9, 1865.

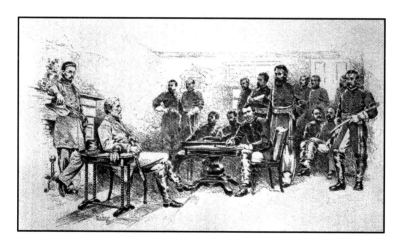

The scene in the parlor of the McLean house as General Robert E. Lee and Lieutenant General Ulysses S. Grant discuss the terms of surrender.

Custer, he handed the souvenir as a gift for the dashing young cavalier's wife.[19] Major General Edward Ord left, carrying the table where Grant had been seated. Others made away with chairs, while others mercilessly cut the caned bottoms out of seats or made off with strips of fabric.[20]

The day after the historic scene at the McLean house, Confederate Brigadier General Edward Porter Alexander took a walk through the small village when he happened upon McLean, a distant relative. Alexander was unaware his relative had moved away from the Manassas area and inquired what he was doing in the village so far from his home at Bull Run. McLean, still very angry over the ordeal, was not too pleasant in his reply: "'What are you doing here?' These armies tore my place on Bull Run all to pieces, and kept running over it backward and forward till no man could live there, so I just sold out and came here, two hundred miles away, hoping I should never see a soldier again. And now, just look around you! Not a fence-rail is left on the place, the last guns trampled down all my crops, and Lee surrenders to Grant in my house."[21] Truly it can be said that the Civil War began in Wilmer McLean's front yard and ended in his front parlor.

Déjà Vu in the Wilderness

During the Battle of Chancellorsville in early May 1863 the Confederacy suffered one of its greatest losses when Stonewall Jackson was mortally wounded by his own men after that general directed a successful flanking attack on the Union army. One year later, on May 6, 1864, disaster struck Lee's Army of Northern Virginia again under strikingly similar circumstances. During the second day of the Battle of the Wilderness, fighting erupted in the early morning hours as Major

General Winfield Scott Hancock's II Corps burst from its entrenchments. Surprised Confederates were pushed back from the Union onslaught. Lieutenant General James Longstreet's I Corps rushed to the scene and reinforced the Rebel defense. With Longstreet's support, the Confederate line rallied and forced the Federals back. After two hours of fighting, the battle lines remained in the same positions they had been in the previous evening.

Confederate scouts examining the terrain ascertained that Hancock's left flank was vulnerable to a turning maneuver similar to the one Stonewall Jackson had performed one year earlier a few miles away at Chancellorsville.[22] To make matters even better, an unfinished railroad bed was found, upon which Longstreet's troops could march, concealed from the unsuspecting Federals.

Four brigades formed the flanking column on the unfinished railroad. Soon the Rebel yell echoed throughout the Wilderness, as the line moved forward on the flank and rear of the Federal left. The Union troops were unprepared for such an attack and were forced to fall back.[23] It was a repeat of Chancellorsville. Years later, with the war just a memory, Hancock, in a conversation with Longstreet, remarked of the attack on his flank at the Wilderness, "You rolled me up like a wet blanket, and it was some hours before I could reorganize for battle."[24]

Longstreet was elated over the effect the attack had produced and began preparing to follow up its success. In his memoirs, he wrote that he rode with Brigadier Generals Micah Jenkins and Joseph Kershaw at his side. "After discussing the dispositions of their troops for reopening the battle, Jenkins rode closer to offer congratulations, saying, 'I am happy; I have felt despair of the cause for some months, but am relieved, and feel assured that we will put the enemy back across the Rapidan before night.' "[25]

As Jenkins said, this musket fire erupted from a Confederate regiment in a wooded area that mistook another nearby Southern regiment for attacking Federal troops. Caught in the fire was Longstreet and his party. In the volley Longstreet was struck in the throat and right shoulder but would eventually recover from these wounds.

Ironically, the events of Longstreet's wounding were strikingly similar to the fatal wounding of Stonewall Jackson. Both events occurred in early May, almost a year to the day apart. Jackson was wounded on May 2, 1863, while Longstreet suffered his wounds on May 6, 1864. Both events occurred almost one mile apart from each other in the Wilderness. In addition both generals had completed successful flanking movements that routed the Union army when they were struck down by friendly fire.

A Pleasant Surprise

Joseph Blackburn, a postwar congressman from Kentucky, had one of the most pleasant experiences any soldier could possibly imagine. During the war, Blackburn served in the Confederate army in the western theater. His experience, which he recalled to a group of congressmen years later, took place while on a Mississippi River steamer.

> "Did I ever tell you," he asked, "a funny thing that happened to me during the war? Well, it was in this way: Four days before I went to the front with my regiment we had a little baby girl. She is now grown, and you always see her with me at any social gathering. Well,

in our army the furloughs came very rarely. When we got into line there was no great chance for a man to go home. It was about three years afterward that a few of us were one night going down the Mississippi on a river steamer. I had been sick and was returning to my command, but pretty well broken up even then. As for money, we did not have any, and the night was hot, as I lay down on the deck, my throat almost parched with dust. Pretty soon a little girl came along with a big glass of lemonade. I tell you it looked good to me. She saw me eyeing it, stopped a minute, looked doubtfully at me, and finally came to my side. 'You look as though you wanted something to drink,' she said, and offered me the glass. It wasn't quite the square thing to do, but I took it and handed it back to her empty. It was like nectar to me. Then I thanked the little creature and sent her away. Soon after, just like every child, she came back leading her mother to the poor soldier. By Jupiter, it was my wife, and the girl was the baby whom I had last seen as a baby but just born. You can image the reunion. They were with my brother's family and happened to be going down the river. That was the only time during the four years' fighting that I saw my wife and baby, and under these circumstances what man would ever forget it?"[26]

Chapter Four

Ghosts

Love's Last Breath

The Battle of Fredericksburg has been recorded as one of the greatest victories for the Army of Northern Virginia. On a cold December day in 1862, some 114,000 Federal troops were flung against 72,500 Confederates stationed on the heights above the city.[1] Many of the casualties occurred when Union troops advanced against a stone wall on Marye's Heights. The result was a disaster for the Northern army, as the wall was never reached. Confederate Major General Lafayette McLaws stated in his report of the battle that "the body of one man, believed to be an officer, was found within 30 yards of the stone wall, and other single bodies were scattered at increased distances until the main mass of the dead lay thickly strewn over the ground at something over 100 yards off. . . ."[2]

During the fighting of December 13, a remarkable incident happened. A strong thread of love extended from Fredericksburg over hundreds of miles north to the small town of Henrietta, New York, where Mrs. Charles Stevenson was at home alone in her yard. Her husband, Charles, was serving as a sergeant in Company G of the 108th New York Infantry. [3]

Mrs. Stevenson probably did not know that a great battle was under way, only that her husband was somewhere south of the Potomac River.

In Henrietta, New York, far away from the guns, Mrs. Stevenson worked in her yard, unaware of the terrible ordeal happening hundreds of miles to the south. Suddenly, she felt a presence behind her. Abruptly, she turned to see who had approached without warning. While turning, she could feel a warm breath of air on her cheek, which startled her even more. Soon fear was replaced with elation as standing in front of her was a vision of her husband, Sergeant Charles Stevenson. She cried out, "Oh! Charlie, is that you?" But, the vision vanished as quickly as it had appeared. Perhaps it was one last look, one last goodbye before Charles left the mortal ground of earth. She quickly returned to the house, knowing she

The stonewall at Fredericksburg.

would never see her husband alive again. All she now had was that one last warm breath of a life she loved so much, a life that was extinguished in front of the stone wall at Fredericksburg.[4]

Coming Home

During the siege of Petersburg, one of the most dangerous places to be was the picket reserve where soldiers were under constant threat of a sharpshooter's bullet. Aside from its inherent danger, the picket reserve was usually a dull place to spend the war. Passing the time while staying alive became a priority, and storytelling was a common way to release the boredom. Men would exchange tall tales, ghost stories, or anything else that came to mind. During their time on the reserve picket, Lieutenant George Halpin of the 116th Pennsylvania Volunteers broke the monotony with a ghost story taken from the time he served with the British army in India. Not to be outdone, Lieutenant Eugene Brady broke in to relate a story of his own:

> You all remember that on Saturday evening, May 2d, at Chancellorsville, the fight was pretty hot for a while, and a good many of our people dropped in the woods on the right of the line? Well, it is one of them that I will tell you. There was an old lady living at that time in the little village of Hockendaque, on the Lehigh River, who had a son in the Eleventh Corps. On Sunday morning May 3d, the old lady crossed the river to Catasauqua, a village just opposite to where she lived, and called upon the pastor of a church, with whom she was acquainted. She told him that her son was home and

walking around the streets, but he would not speak to her. "Last evening (Saturday)," said she, "I was washing out some things, the door was open, and who should walk in but my son John. I did not expect him, and I was so astonished for a moment, I did not realize his presence, then quickly drying my hands on my apron, I ran towards him. Would you believe it, he never offered to come towards me but, giving me such a sad, strange look, and without uttering a word, he turned and walked up the stairs. As soon as I could come to my senses I ran after him, but he was gone. The window was open and he must have climbed down the trellis-work that the grape-vine clings to, and so left the house. I lay awake all night thinking, and expecting him to come back, but daylight came and no John. I got the breakfast and started to hunt him up, and as I was walking along the street I saw my son just in front of me. I ran to catch up but he turned a corner, and when I reached there he was gone. I dare say he went into one of the neighbor's houses, but which one I could not find out. Now, sir, you can see that my son is evidently angry at something and will not speak to me. Won't you come over to Hockendaque to see him, and find out what is the matter?" The reverend gentleman, pitying the poor woman, returned with her to her home, hoping to find her boy and have mother and son reconciled. He hunted everywhere through the village, but could learn nothing of the soldier. No one had seen him but his mother. On Tuesday morning, May 5th, a letter came saying that the boy had been killed on Saturday evening, just at the time that he walked in to see his mother. [5]

The Ghosts of Cedar Creek

Clifton Johnson recorded the following story which took place on the Cedar Creek battlefield in the Shenandoah Valley, Virginia. At the battle of Cedar Creek, Virginia, the Confederate Army of the Valley, led by Lieutenant General Jubal Early, launched a surprise attack upon the Union Army of the Shenandoah, commanded by Major General Philip Sheridan. The Union army was in a retreat until a counterattack was organized that in turn routed the Confederate army, winning the day for the Federals. Clifton Johnson recorded this story as told by a former slave who lived near the Cedar Creek battlefield and proceeded to publish this story in his book *Battleground Adventures*, in 1915:

> . . . Right after the war we used to hear the soldiers ghos'es shootin' hyar all aroun' on the battlefield, and we'd hear horses in the back lane comin' klopity, klopity, klopity. The horses would ride right up to you, but you could n't see a thing.

Cedar Creek battlefield.

I know one man who lived out on a farm and he come in to the town one night to pra'r meetin'. As he was goin' home 'bout ten o'clock he heard the bugle and the rap of the kittle drum. While he was listenin' he seen a officer a-walkin' ahead of a squad of soldiers. The officers hollered "Halt!" to 'em, and they stopped. But the bugle kep' a-blowin', and pretty soon they marched off.

Thar was another man who used to come to town pretty nigh every night, and some of the nights was tolerable dark. He was co'tin' hyar, I allow. Many a night he'd hear horses comin' cross the fields, and canteens and swords hittin' the sides of saddles, blangity, blangity, blangity!

Down near Cedar Crick thar's a ghos' in a barn. The ghos' is supposed to be a soldier that was killed tharabouts. He has Yankee clothes on and wears cavalry boots that come way up to his knees. Some say he has no head, and others say he has a head and wears a plug hat. People see him after night, jus' about dusk, and he only comes at that time of the evening. He walks out of the haymow and part way down the haymow steps, and thar he'll stan'. For one while the railroad ran excursion trains so people could come and see the ghos'. I went thar to see him once, but I was 'fraid to go into the barn.

The first person who ever seen the ghos' was a farmer by the name of Holt Hottel who had rented the place. He went to feed his horses jus' after sundown and was goin' to throw some hay down the hole to the feedingroom when he noticed the ghos'. But he thought it was a tramp, and he says, "Git out of hyar. I don't allow tramps in the barn on account of fire."

The ghos' did n't say anything and jus' stood thar. Holt got mad then and tried to gouge the ghos' with his pitchfork, and the fork went right through the ghos' into the weather-boarding. That was evidence it was n't no tramp, and Holt jumped right down the hole into the feeding-room. His horses did n't git no hay that night, and for a good while afterward he fed 'em tolerable early.

Holt's father used to laugh at him 'bout that ghos', but one evenin' Holt met the ol' man comin' from the barn as hard as he could run. Oh! he was comin' from thar skatin'. He did n't laugh at Holt no mo'.

Another time a black man who'd gone to the barn a little late to feed the stock came out of there a-hustlin', and he was whoopin' as if he was goin' to be killed.

But the ghos' did nobaody no harm, and Holt got so he'd go in thar any time of the night. He become accustomed to seeing this thing and paid no attention to it. Once when he threshed his wheat the grain was too damp to put in sacks, and he left it on the barn floor a few days to dry. Thar was some danger that it would be stolen, and he stayed in the barn nights to guard it and slept on an ol' lounge he carried out from the house. He said that night after night he went to sleep with that feller standin' on the haymow steps. He seen him perfectly plain even to the straps on his boots what he hooked his fingers in to pull 'em on.

Thar's people who have tried all sorts of ways to see that ghos' and never could, and thar's plenty of others who have seen it. I know this—that Holt Hottel was a reliable a man thar was in the state. His word was as good as his bond.[6]

Chapter Five

Dreams

The Spotted Hand

The Civil War was not born during April 1861. Its embers smoldered for many years prior to that fateful April when they burst into the flames of war. One issue that fanned these flames was the tariff question. The tariff, or what some called the "American System," was originally designed to provide revenue for a fledgling national treasury. However, as the country grew, the tariff became a tool for protectionism. Manufacturing interests in the North wanted protection from foreign competition, which would allow them to grow and prosper. By adding a tariff to imported products, the price of these products would be higher, making domestic goods more desirable for the American consumer. Those states with an agricultural economy opposed the tariff system since they did not have a strong manufacturing ability and imported many items from abroad.

By 1828 the tariff question had mushroomed into political turmoil. Southern leaders began to openly speak of a state's right to nullify Federal law. Some were so bold as to use the floor of Congress for such action. The situation came to a climax with the Tariff Act of 1832. In response to this legislation, South Carolina convened and passed an Ordinance of Nullification. The ordinance forbade all authorities within the borders of South Carolina to enforce the payment of duties imposed by the tariff laws. South Carolina had laid down the gauntlet and was defying the Constitution.

After a proclamation by President Andrew Jackson against the Ordinance of Nullification, South Carolina took steps to carry on with its opposition of Federal law by calling out the militia and ordering war supplies. Jackson, a former general and hero of the Battle of New Orleans, would not be threatened. He vowed to uphold the Constitution and issued orders for troops to proceed to Charleston along with a war ship to insure the tariff would be collected. Realizing that Jackson was unyielding in his commitment to carry out Federal law, South Carolina reconsidered her position and the nullification ordinance. Jackson also lent a hand in addressing the grievances of the Southern states by having a bill introduced into Congress reducing the tariff. After lengthy debate and amendments, the "Clay Compromise" was enacted, reducing the tariff over a period of 10 years. Sectional difficulties were postponed for a time, but not solved for at least 30 years, when it would then cost the nation a high price in blood.

One of the leading figures in the Nullification standoff was John Calhoun, vice president under Andrew Jackson. While serving as vice president, Calhoun publicly advocated nullification. As the tariff crisis grew, in 1832 Calhoun resigned the vice presidency, and he quickly returned to the nation's capital as Senator Calhoun, taking up the fight for nullification and states' rights in general. In fact, it was Senator

Calhoun who spoke loudest when the rights of South Carolina and her sister states were threatened.[1]

* * * * *

The following article was written in the *Evening Post* during the time of the Nullification Crisis. It recounts a dream Senator Calhoun had late one night as he pondered the future of the state he so very much loved and its relationship with the remainder of the country:

> At a late hour last night, as I was sitting in my room, engaged in writing, I was astonished by the entrance of a visitor who, without a word, took a seat opposite me at my table. This surprised me, as I had given particular orders to the servant that I should on no account be disturbed. The manner in which the intruder entered, so perfectly self-possessed, taking his seat opposite me without a word, as though my room and all within it belonged to him, excited in me as much surprise as indignation. As I raised my head to look into his features, over the top of my shaded lamp, I discovered that he was wrapped in a thin cloak, which effectually concealed his face and features from my view; and as I raised my head, he spoke: "What are you writing, senator from South Carolina?" I did not think of his impertinence at first, but answered him voluntarily, "I am writing a plan for the dissolution of the American Union.". . . To this the intruder replied, in the coolest manner possible, "Senator from South Carolina, will you allow me to look at your hand, your right hand?" He rose, the cloak fell, and I beheld his face. . . . It was the face of a dead man, whom extraordinary events had called back to life.

The features were those of General George Washington. . . . The intruder, as I have said, rose and asked to look at my right hand, as though I had not the power to refuse. I extended it. The truth is, I felt a strange thrill pervade me at his touch; he grasped it and held it near the light, thus affording full time to examine every feature. It was the face of Washington. After holding my hand for a moment, he looked at me steadily, and said in a quiet way, "And with this right hand[,] senator from South Carolina, you would sign your name to a paper declaring the Union dissolved?" I answered in the affirmative. "Yes," I said, "if a certain contingency arises, I will sign my name to the Declaration of Dissolution." But at that moment a black blotch appeared on the back of my hand. . . . "That," said he, dropping my hand, "is the mark by which Benedict Arnold is known in the next world." He said no more, gentlemen, but drew from beneath his cloak an object which he laid upon the table—laid upon the very paper upon which I was writing. This object, gentlemen was a skeleton. "There," said he, "there are the bones of Isaac Hayne, who was hung at Charleston by the British. He gave his life in order to establish the Union. When you put your name to a Declaration of Dissolution, why, you may as well have the bones of Isaac Hayne before you—he was a South Carolinian and so are you. But there was no blotch on his right hand." With these words the intruder left the room. I started back from the contact with the dead man's bones and—awoke. . . .[2]

"Just What I Dreamed"

On March 25, 1865, Private D. W. Dare of the 10th Vermont Infantry, Company H found himself on picket duty in front of Petersburg.[3] The "picket-line was composed of about 160 men of the Fourteenth New Jersey on the right and 230 of the Tenth Vermont on the left, the whole line being nearly one mile in length, with open ground on the right half, while the left portion of the line was immediately in rear of a narrow belt of woods. The picket-line of the enemy was strongly intrenched behind earth-works and at an average distance of 300 yards."[4]

While on duty, Private Dare had a surprise visit from his tent mate, Private Joe Smith, who was upset and ventured out to the picket line to talk. During their conversation, Joe revealed a disturbing dream he had earlier that morning. The following story is Private Dare's rendition of his friend's dream:

> While encamped in front of Petersburg we lay near Fort Fisher. I had three tentmates, Sergt. E. T. Johnson, Joseph A. Smith, and John Smith. John Smith was a quiet Irishman, with dry, humorous wit, the trio making a very pleasant set of mates, and many evenings have we passed in soldier life in pleasant converse together. Joseph had been home on a sick furlough, and while in hospital he became acquainted with a young lady, and perhaps was engaged when he returned to the front, which was but a few days previous to what I am about to relate.
>
> On the morning of the 25th of March, '65 our regiment, the 10th Vt., were detailed for picket. We had been on the picket line but a short time when Joe Smith

came to me and said he had a dream that troubled him, and wished to relate it; so we sat down, and he said he dreamed we were going to advance the picket line; we should have a hard fight, and that he and John would be killed, but I should get through safe. I laughed at him and told him there was no indication of an engagement, and he must not trouble himself about dreams, but he continued and said he wanted I should pack his things and send them home, designating the disposition of the articles, particularly a ring he wore.

While talking, what should we see but Colonel [George] Damon coming through the main line on horseback, towards our line. Says Joe, "There, Dan, that is just what I dreamed." The colonel came down and told us we must take the rebel picket line in our front, but go no further; to pack up carefully so the rebs would not see us, and at a signal from Fort Fisher, charge the line. Joe was quite sad and told me to keep near him. We got the order to go, and started through an open field, had not gone more than twenty-five rods before the rebs opened on us and [with] the first volley Joe fell, shot through the groin, severing the main artery. As I seized him the blood spurted all over me, and I could not stop it, the ball passing clear through him producing a wound that must soon end in death. He lingered a short time with his head resting in my arms, telling me to be sure to send his effects home as before requested.

Meantime the troops not having started with our regiment, we were ordered back, but I remained out in the open field until Joe breathed his last—being safe from the enemy's fire while caring for a wounded comrade. I took the ring from the dead soldier's finger and made a lively retreat down the hill through a shower of bullets, to the right, into a swamp, thinking to get out of range. I found John Smith behind a stump all in a heap. Says I, "Why don't you fall back?" "In faith I'll wait until they come again and save so much travel." Just then five or six rebs fired at the sound of our voices; one ball cut my sleeve from my elbow to wrist, and one cut a furrow through the top of John's head, killing him almost instantly. The dream was verified. I was safe thus far. I fell back to the line. . . .[5]

As the initial assault failed, two Ohio regiments, the 122nd and 110th, were ordered forward to support the attack. At the double-quick they ran with fixed bayonets. The line surged through the field toward the Confederate works. Before long they too encountered severe musketry fire. Then Rebel artillery from the rear joined the battle. Round shot and shells started to tear huge gaps into the line. The blue wave crossed half the field when the fire on their flanks grew unbearable. Orders were given and the line retreated. Four more regiments—the 67th Pennsylvania, 9th New York Heavy Artillery, 6th Maryland, and 126th Ohio—were brought forward to reinforce the second attack.[6]

At four o'clock a flag from Fort Fisher gave the signal.[7] The Union line swept forward. This time they would not be denied. Running at the double-quick, the men held their fire. A loud cheer arose as the blue lines carried the entrenched Rebel works. Finally the Federals stopped and poured a volley of musketry into their gray adversaries. Confederate resistance, overwhelmed by the charge, quickly dissipated. Many threw down their weapons and surrendered at the onslaught.

During the charge the 10th Vermont captured 160 prisoners. There were only two fatalities: Privates John Smith and Joseph Smith. Private John Smith had to endure death twice, as his dream or perhaps more fittingly, his nightmare, came true.[8]

Nightmare of Home

Colonel Warren Akin served the Confederacy not as a soldier but as a Representative from Georgia in the Confederate Congress. While living in Richmond, Colonel Akin was not physically in harm's way, but the agony of being separated from one's family during wartime was present. During the late fall of 1864, Colonel Akin was tortured with a nightmare so vivid it seemed real. He dreamed of the chinaberry-tree that stood next to his house in Elberton, Georgia. Lying at its base was his oldest son. The boy showed no sign of movement and his head rested in a pool of blood. In the dream the colonel saw himself running toward his son to see whether he was still alive. Gently, he raised the boy up by the hand, as blood ran from his right ear.

As Akin awoke in his Richmond residence, he shook off his sleep and quickly traveled to the nearest telegraph office. He had to know immediately whether there was trouble at home. Unfortunately, like so many things in Richmond during the winter of 1865, using the telegraph wasn't easy. The wires had been cut, possibly by Union forces that were constantly pressuring the city. A frantic Akin quickly arranged to depart for his home in Elberton. However, before he had a chance to leave, a letter arrived from his wife informing him that all was well. Colonel Akin was relieved from his dreadful fear and went about resuming business as usual.

Three weeks passed when Akin received another letter from home. This time the news wasn't cheerful. Instead, it confirmed Akin's dream. The letter stated that his son had fallen from a horse, hitting his head against a chinaberry-tree. The boy lay unconscious, while a neighbor rushed to help. Picking the boy up by the arm the neighbor noticed blood flowing from his right ear. The fallen youth held on for three days before he died. The events occurred just like in the dream of Colonel Akins, only this time the feeling of sadness was ever so real and ever so unshakable.[9]

Jenkins' Troubling Dream

The men of General James Longstreet's I Corps received good news on April 18, 1864—they were going back east to rejoin the Confederate Army of Northern Virginia. The I Corps had been temporarily detached to the Army of Tennessee in order to assist against Union forces under command of Major General William Rosecrans.[10]

One man that was certainly happy with the move was Brigadier General Micah Jenkins, who was tired of the frustrating and disappointing campaign. In addition Jenkins had been troubled by haunting dreams where he saw himself riding into battle but not riding out. Before returning to the Army of Northern Virginia, Jenkins paid a visit to his wife, Carrie. This was the first chance the couple had to be together since they lost their newborn son to fever the previous fall.[11] Before the visit ended, Jenkins revealed to his wife the troubling dreams he had.[12] Back with the army Jenkins met Colonel Asbury Coward, one of his closest friends. During one of their visits Jenkins informed his friend of another dream. In this one he could see his entire life until the next battle, when the dream became blank. Jenkins inquired of his friend, "Why have I not forgotten this dream, as I have all the others I've had before? . . . It's as clear and the details are as sharp as though I actually lived it."[13]

Back with the Army of Northern Virginia, Jenkins had little time to wonder about his dreams and their meanings as the war stirred from its winter hibernation. In early May the Union Army of the Potomac crossed the Rapidan River and headed toward Richmond. Within days the Battle of the Wilderness began, as the Federals pushed through the thick tangle of brush and trees only to bump into the waiting Army of Northern Virginia.

On the second day of the battle, May 6, the situation looked grim for the Southern army. Union Major General Winfield Hancock's Federal troops had surged forth from their entrenchments, hitting the battle-weary Rebels at first light. The Confederate line wavered and bent rapidly. A Confederate countercharge broke the Union momentum.

About this time Longstreet's Corps arrived from Gordonsville where it had spent the winter. The addition of these troops helped to stabilize the battleline to the point where they had begun earlier in the morning.[14] Longstreet immediately turned his attention to the possibility of flanking the Union line by using an unfinished railroad that connected Gordonsville and Fredericksburg to cover the movement. Four brigades quietly assembled on the railroad bed and waited to move forward. Soon the Rebel yell echoed through the Wilderness, and the gray line advanced on the unsuspecting Federals. "The movement was a complete surprise and a perfect success. It was executed with rare zeal and intelligence. The enemy made but a short stand, and fell back, in utter rout with heavy loss, to a position about three-quarters of a mile from my front attack," reported Longstreet.[15]

Jenkins' men were held in reserve and waited for the order to proceed down the Orange Plank Road. Longstreet, flush with victory, rode at the head of the men, joined by Jenkins and Brigadier General Joseph Kershaw and staff. The meeting had an air of triumph as well as business. The successful assault quickly needed to be followed with another to keep the Union line on the run. As the men rode forward, plans were made and troop dispositions discussed. Jenkins was delighted at the outcome of the movement, riding closer to Longstreet and offering his congratulations: "I am happy; I have felt despair of the cause for some months, but am relieved, and feel assured that we will put the enemy back across the Rapidan before night."[16] As the group continued to ride, they crossed the path of the 12th Virginia Infantry. Suddenly

Confederate forces capture a breastworks during the fighting of May 6, 1864, in the Wilderness.

Courtesy *Battles and Leaders of the Civil War*

shots rang out and the Virginians threw themselves upon the ground to avoid the fire from the Southern battle line. Their retrograde movement had been mistaken for an advance of Union infantry. At this very time Longstreet and Jenkins rode into the volley of musketry. Jenkins had barely finished speaking when he was hit.[17] The brigadier fell from his horse, striking the ground.[18] At the same

Brigadier General Micah Jenkins, killed at the Battle of the Wilderness, May 6, 1864.

Courtesy *Battles and Leaders of the Civil War*

time Longstreet received a minie ball in the throat and right shoulder. In response, the soldiers in Jenkins' Brigade immediately leveled their guns to return the volley. Kershaw called out that they were "Friends," and the men recovered their arms before any more harm was done.[19]

Jenkins lay on the ground. The missile had penetrated his forehead and lodged in the brain. His friend, Asbury Coward, heard of the sad news and arrived immediately. Taking Jenkins by the hand, he attempted to arouse his friend. "Jenkins, . . . Mike, do you know me?"[20] Jenkins was only able to exert a little pressure on Coward's hand. His body then convulsed and lay quiet. Later that afternoon, at about 5 P.M., the young brigadier died. Micah Jenkins' questions about his dream were answered.

Chapter Six

Natural Wonders

The War Comets

Since the beginning of time, comets have been associated with prophetic signs of impending disaster. During the year 1861, the skies over the United States were visited by several comets, including the Thatcher and Tebbutt Comets. For anyone that was superstitious and knew how tense national politics were in April of 1861, the arrival of the Thatcher had to be a clue of impending war.[1]

In *Tad Lincoln's Father*, Julia Taft Bayne recalls how an old slave woman, Oola, viewed the comet as a dire prediction:

. . . "You see dat great fire sword, blazin' in de sky," she said. "Dat's a great war comin' and de handle's to'rd de Norf and de point to'rd de Souf and de Norf's gwine take dat sword and cut de Souf's heart out. But dat Linkum man, chilluns, if he takes de sword, he's gwine perish by it." . . .

. . . We told the Lincoln boys about Oola's prophecy of war, carefully omitting, however, the dire prediction regarding their father. Tad was greatly impressed and carried the story, as tidings of import, to his father.

Mrs. Lincoln laughed, but the President seemed strangely interested.

"What was that, Tad, that she said about the comet?" asked Mr. Lincoln.

"She said," answered Tad, gratified that at least one member of his family appreciated the gravity of the omen, "that the handle was toward the north and the point toward the south and that meant the north was going to take that sword and cut the South's heart out. Do you think that's what it means, Pa?"

"I hope not, Tad," answered his father gravely. "I hope it won't come to that."[2]

Oola's prediction of a "great war comin'" certainly was fulfilled. However, in April 1861 nobody knew which direction that fiery sword in the sky was pointing, north or south. As for Lincoln, Oola's prediction would certainly become an ever-burdening mystery as the war wore on.

* * * * *

Tebbutt's Comet was the second comet to appear in 1861.[3] Because it appeared totally unexpectedly, it caused more excitement than the Thatcher Comet. The *New York Herald* described its June 30 appearance as "Unheralded and unnoticed, it has burst upon us with all its heavenly beauty."[4] A worker at the Allegheny Observatory stated in the *Philadelphia Daily Evening Bulletin* that "his hair stood up with wonder and excitement. There was nothing of its description in the books; nothing in any late astronomical calculations anywhere which would lead one to expect the appearance of any such celestial stranger, and moreover, while the approach of comets is gradual, growing more and more brilliant, this one

has burst suddenly into view in all its full effulgence."[5] The
American Journal of Science and Arts agreed, stating, "We must
conclude then that this comet is a new one, whose orbit has
never before been computed."[6]

Not only did Tebbutt's sudden appearance fascinate ob-
servers, but its extraordinary brightness and size intrigued
almost everyone who witnessed its journey. It was described
as "having a head as large as the full moon and a tail that
stretched half way across the nighttime sky."[7] When compared to others, Tebbutt's Comet was considered to be "one
of the most brilliant comets of the last fifty years."[8]

At the time Tebbutt's Comet was visiting the skies over
the United States, the bombardment of Fort Sumter was already two-and-a-half months in the past. During this period
events were slow to unfold, as both sides prepared for what
many thought would be a short one-battle war. Federal forces
marched into Washington and camped in the fields around
the city. Just a few miles south, in Virginia, Rebel volunteers
gathered. Each side trained their men in the art of warfare
and waited for the first Union advance on Richmond.

An article in the July 3 edition of the *Philadelphia Daily
Evening Bulletin* summed up how one person felt as he witnessed the nightly spectacle:

> We could not but think how strangely this pale visi-
> tant must look to our encamped legions at the South,
> as they viewed it from between their tents in the open
> fields of Virginia and Maryland. How they must have
> speculated upon it at their pickets, and as they lay
> around their canvas houses, while the solemn proces-
> sion of the stars moved on, and the unfamiliar sounds
> of the night struck upon their ears. They must have

filled up the night watches with reveries on all the poetry about comets which Shakespeare affords, and they doubtless made their astronomical acquirements stretch as far as they were able in puzzling over the origin and appearance of this unexpected celestial visitor.[9]

Another contributor of editorial space, this time in the July 4 *New York Times,* entitled his piece "The Red Avenger of the North—the Comet Seen July 2, 1861." In the letter the writer describes the comet and its placement in the sky. However, the last paragraph sums up the letter with a dire prediction for the Southern people: "Not having seen any prediction published of this comet, I was much surprised, as no doubt thousands of others were. Can't some of our astronomers enlighten us? Let our Southern friends beware of this, our new ally, for it is coming at 'em."[10]

Just weeks after the sudden appearance of one of the century's greatest comets, the Civil War began in earnest as Federal forces under Brigadier General Irvin McDowell advanced toward Richmond. This time the prophetic power of comets was correct, as they hailed the beginning of America's worst national disaster.

A Heavenly Army

Our senses provide us with the pleasure of sight, sound, smell, taste, and touch, but can be easily deceived at times. For example weather can play tricks with our senses. Cloud formations or heat rising off a desert floor can cause us to question our perceptions. One such phenomenon was witnessed a few miles west of Lewisburg, Greenbrier County, Virginia, on October 1, 1863. Mr. Moses Dwye was seated on his porch enjoying the cool autumn afternoon. He was in the company of five other people, including several women and a servant girl. At about three o'clock they witnessed a strange phenomenon unfolding in the clouds south of the house. This strange cloud formation was remarkable enough to warrant publication in a Southern newspaper:

> The weather was quite hot and dry; not a cloud could be seen; no wind even ruffled the foliage on the surrounding trees. All things being propitious, the grand panorama began to move. Just over and through the tops of the trees on the adjacent hills, to the south, immense numbers of rolls, resembling cotton or smoke, apparently of the size and shape of doors, seemed to be passing rapidly through the air, yet in beautiful order and regularity. The rolls seemed to be tinged on the edge with light green, so as to resemble a border of deep fringe. There were apparently thousands of them; they were perhaps an hour in getting by. After they had passed over and out of sight, the scene was changed from the air above to the earth beneath, and became more intensely interesting to the spectators who were witnessing the panorama from different standpoints.
>
> In the deep valley beneath, thousands upon thousands of (apparently) human beings (men) came in view, traveling in the same direction as the rolls, marching in good order, some thirty or forty in depth, moving rapidly—"double-quick"—and commenced ascending the almost insurmountable hills opposite, and had the stoop peculiar to men ascending a steep mountain. There seemed to be a great variety in the size of the men; some

were very large, whilst others were quite small. Their arms, legs, and heads could be distinctly seen in motion. They seemed to observe strict military discipline, and there were no stragglers.

There was uniformity of dress; white blouses or shirts, with white pants; they were without guns, swords, or anything that indicated "men of war." On they came through the valley and over the steep road, crossing the road, and finally passing out of sight, in a direction due north from those who were looking on.[11]

A Mirage in the Clouds

Years after the war, another phenomenon was witnessed in the clouds of the Dakota Territory. The weather was cold and damp, with fog lying heavy on the ground. Fort Abraham Lincoln was astir with activity. Troopers of the United States Seventh Cavalry were on the move. As the band played "Garry Owen," the mounted men paraded through the fort. Loved ones watched, proud and anxious about the expedition to come. General George Armstrong Custer, dressed in buckskin, was everywhere as the pageant unfolded. Beside him rode his wife, Elizabeth, who would accompany her husband until the next morning, when the two would depart. She would go back to Fort Lincoln and he set off in search of the Sioux Indian. It was a hard parting for the couple but especially for Elizabeth, or "Libbie" as her husband so fondly called her.[12] This was not the first time she bid him farewell, but it was different. "With my husband's departure, my last happy days in garrison were ended; as a premonition of disaster that I had never known before weighted me down. I could not shake off the baleful influence of depressing thoughts."[13] Adding to her apprehension was an illusion she witnessed the morning of their departing. She wrote later, "a mirage appeared which took up about half of the line of cavalry, and thenceforth for a little distance it marched, equally plain to the sight on the earth and in the sky."[14]

Elizabeth didn't know at the time, but her feelings would turn out to be all too true. It was the last time she waved goodbye. Her husband, who had won his first laurels fighting the battles of the Army of the Potomac, rode toward his destiny to a place called the Little Bighorn.

Providence Spring

Civil War prisons were places of death and despair where the lives of their captives were literally destroyed. Many times shelter was limited or even nonexistent, causing men to be exposed to the cold, heat, or rain. Food was often scarce, and prisoners developed scurvy due to the lack of vitamin C in their diet. For those men who managed to survive the prison camp, ailments contracted during their imprisonment would have life-long effects on them, and in some cases, cause premature death. Camp Sumter was one such prisoner-of-war camp, located near the small village of Andersonville, Georgia. Established on February 23, 1864, Camp Sumter was host to over thirteen thousand Union prisoners within three months of its establishment. During this time period, 1,026 deaths occurred, leading to the reputation of Camp Sumter as one of the worst prisons of the war.[15] By the time of its closure, some thirteen thousand Union men would be laid in the prison's cemetery.

Originally, the grounds were built in the pattern of a square and encompassed 17 acres of land to accommodate

10,000 prisoners. In June 1864 the stockade was enlarged to 27 acres and would eventually house over 32,000 Union men.

Descriptions of newcomers to Andersonville compared the prison camp to hell itself. Private W. B. Smith, who made his home in the prison for several months, wrote upon entering the prison that

> . . . we marched to the center of this literal valley of destruction and halted we were engulfed in an ocean of black, grimy, emaciated beings, covered with sores, vermin, rags, matted hair, and weak, strange-sounding voices, crowed around us inquiring about Grant and Sherman, about news of exchange, and wanting to know if we had any hard-tack or coffee to trade for corn bread. Could it be possible, we thought, that these gaunt, filthy creatures, with half-naked, bony limbs, lusterless eyes, and feeble voices, some of them in their starving condition having lost their minds, were ever able-bodied Union soldiers? . . . I never felt so utterly depressed, crushed, and God-forsaken in all my life before.[16]

One area of deep concern for the prison population was the need for clean drinking water. A stream named Sweetwater

Inside Andersonville prison where the dead line can be seen on the far right.

Creek ran under the stockade and through the prison grounds.[17] However, a considerable area of land along the stream was low and boggy, causing the water to become foul.[18] The stream was also used by the prisoners for toilet purposes and further polluted by "washings from the cook house and the Confederate camps."[19] Private W. B. Smith related in his memoirs that this area "emitted a sickening odor, and the old prisoners told us to keep away from it as far as possible for fear of gangrene."[20]

Since the water of Sweetwater Creek was so polluted, prisoners had to obtain drinking water elsewhere. The only other means of procuring a suitable drink were wells dug by the prisoners. Sometimes these had to be quite deep, causing the ground to cave in, making it quite difficult to harvest the precious liquid.[21] This changed on one sultry afternoon as the hand of God would deliver an oasis in the middle of their desert of misery to the lost souls of Andersonville.

The days of the 7th, 8th, and 9th of August 1864 were some of the hottest in Andersonville history. For the prisoners, this heat was not simply an inconvenience, but a death trap with no way out. During the three days a total of five hundred men perished. Relief finally came on the last day when a storm broke upon the land. John Urban, a prisoner, wrote:

> the large ink-black clouds approaching from the West, the constant vivid flashes of lightning, and sharp, quick claps of thunder, which reminded us of a heavy cannonade, all indicated that a fearful storm was approaching, and we watched its approach with a great deal of interest and anxiety. It was not pleasant in our unsheltered condition to be exposed to such a terrible storm as this threatened to be, but then we needed a

heavy rain so badly that we were rather glad to see its approach. It soon burst over us with a fury that was appalling, and the rain poured down as if all the floodgates of the heavens had opened. The deluge of water, the terrific flashes of lightning, the crashes of thunder and roaring of the storm, made a scene awful and grand; and it seemed as if all the elements of heaven were combining to set us free. The lightning struck into the stockade, and several times into the trees that surrounded our prison in rapid succession, and the prisoners to shut out the terrible sight sat down on the ground and covered their faces with their hands.[22]

The next day the rains returned, bringing more relief from the Georgia heat. On the third day the prisoners were greeted with cool and pleasant weather. In addition to the relief from the heat the rain had served to wash away the filth

A mass of Union prisoners as viewed from the main gate of Andersonville prison.

that littered the ground and even cleaned the swamp of much its debris. What truly amazed the prisoners was the sight of water—clean, clear water gurgling from the ground. In the midst of the downpour a spring erupted between the dead line and stockade about one hundred yards up the slope from Sweetwater Creek. Men whose thoughts wondered how God could ever allow them to suffer in such a place had renewed faith. The spring was truly a gift from heaven and was named "Providence Spring" in honor of the kind Providence who had sent it.[23]

With Charity for All

Inaugural Day in Washington, 1865, could have almost been a celebration of victory. Certainly it was a far cry from Lincoln's first, when death threats and rumors of war abounded and the city seemed "anxious and depressed." Throughout the four years Lincoln had proven himself capable of leading the nation. He was no longer a "long, lean, sallow frontier lawyer". . . who used "homely phrases and mispronunciations." He was now, truly, the leader of the people.[24]

The day did not start like a celebration, rather it began "dark and drizzly."[25] Storm clouds rumbled through the city, shaking buildings and people to the core like some great battle in the sky. The ceremonies commenced in a packed Senate chamber away from the rain. At about noon the vice president elect, Andrew Johnson, began his speech. It was a total disaster. Having taken a little too much whiskey to calm his nerves, the vice president elect gave "a rambling, incoherent address which shocked many" in the crowd.[26] After Johnson was sworn in, the newly elected senators took their vow to uphold the Constitution. By this time the storms of the morning had ceased and the ceremony was moved outside for the swearing in of the president.

As Lincoln appeared on the eastern side of the Capitol building, the great man was greeted by thousands of people, many standing in ankle deep mud, anticipating the historic occasion. Suddenly, "the mist and the clouds cleared away, and the sun shone out bright and warm. The atmosphere seemed unusually clear."[27] It was almost as if God spoke to the people and proclaimed that the storm was over and only the light of peace was before them.

Lincoln did not disappoint the crowd as he gave a short address. His historic words of forgiveness would be immortalized in history when he pledged "with malice towards none; with charity for all."[28] He then turned to Chief Justice Salmon P. Chase and took the oath of office. After the oath was administered, the president leaned forward and kissed the Bible, as a salute of artillery echoed across the city.

Sergeant Smith Stimmel, a member of the Union Light Guard and one of Lincoln's personal escorts, recorded the event as Lincoln's carriage pulled away from the Capitol building:

> Soon after the president concluded his address, he entered his carriage, and the procession started up Pennsylvania Avenue to the White House, the escort from our company following next to his carriage.
>
> Shortly after we turned onto Pennsylvania Avenue, west of the Capitol, I noticed the crowd along the street looking intently, and some were pointing to something in the heavens toward the south. I glanced up in that direction, and there in plain view, shining out in all her

starlike beauty, was the planet Venus. It was a little after midday at the time I saw it, possibly near one o'clock; the sun seemed to be a little west of the meridian, the star a little east.

It was a strange sight. I never saw a star at that time in the day before or since. The superstitious had many strange notions about it, but of course it was simply owing to the peculiarly clear condition of the atmosphere and the favorable position of the planet at that time. The President and those who were with him in the carriage noticed the star at the same time.[29]

It was a great day in America, the land of the free. Forgiveness was offered and soon the sword would be turned into a plowshare. But, even as the warmth of the bright sunlight on that glorious day pushed away the clouds of war and Venus shone brightly, an evil lurked nearby, an evil that would not forgive nor be forgiven, but one that would seek its time and place to do the unthinkable. There watching was the actor John Wilkes Booth.

Chapter Seven

Dumb Luck

Hits and Misses with the Big Guns

When picturing an assault during the Civil War, one's idea turns to rows of infantry running with bayonets glistening in the sun against waiting cannon. The big gun's lanyard is pulled and canister is thrown from the muzzle. Like a giant shotgun, the missiles pour forth and anything in their way is decimated.

This scene or ones similar to it occurred on many Civil War battlefields. As deadly and awesome as Civil War artillery was, artillery projectiles, especially round shot, were deceptive in their speed. Edward Anderson, colonel of the 19th Indiana Cavalry, took some advice to heart that his grandfather, a veteran of the War of 1812, had given him: "Never try to stop a cannon-ball."[1] Anderson at first thought his grandfather was being a little overcautious until he witnessed one of the iron balls roll along the ground and take off a sapling without its progress being materially checked.

One Wisconsin soldier should have heeded this type of advice when he tried his luck at stopping a ball as it rolled by him on the first day at Gettysburg. Unfortunately, he was surprised as the ball took off his leg and kept rolling on its way.[2] In another incident during that first day, Captain Robert Story of Company B, 76th New York Infantry, received a close call when a ball rolled between his legs without doing any injury. However, his luck ran out when just a few minutes later he was struck by a minie ball in the left thigh, fracturing the bone. Captain Story eventually succumbed to his injury and died on August 6.[3]

No Place to Hide

Not all casualties of artillery were caused by direct hits or balls rolling along on the ground. One such casualty occurred at Spotsylvania Courthouse in May 1864. A Northern infantryman, exhausted from battle, sought shelter behind a tree. Standing with his back against his wooden fortification, the man relaxed as much as one can during the ordeal of battle. Suddenly a solid shot hit the trunk about four feet from the ground. The ball did not have enough force to tear

Union artillery showing a field gun and mortar.

Courtesy *Battles and Leaders of the Civil War*

through the wood, but the soldier fell dead without a scratch, the result of a concussion.[4]

Too Close for Comfort

Other incidents occurred with round shot, which seemed hard to predict where it was going and what it would do when it got there. Lieutenant Frank Haskell, who served on Major General John Gibbon's staff, recorded the following incidents, which took place during the cannonade prior to Major General George Pickett's famous charge at Gettysburg:

> We saw a man coming up from the rear with his full knapsack on, and some canteens of water held by the straps, in his hands. He was walking slowly and with apparent unconcern, though the iron hailed around him. A shot struck the knapsack, and it and its contents flew thirty yards in every direction,—the knapsack disappeared like an egg, thrown spitefully against a rock. The soldier stopped, and turned about in puzzled surprise, —put up one hand to his back to assure himself that the knapsack was not there, and then walked slowly on again unharmed, with not even his coat torn.[5]

Haskell goes on to tell of a frightened soldier who was

> . . . crouching behind a small disintegrated stone, which was about the size of a common water-bucket. He was bent up, with his face to the ground, in the attitude of a pagan worshiper, before his idol. It looked so absurd to see him thus, that I went and said to him: "Do not lie there like a toad—Why not go to your regiment and be a man?" He turned up his face with a stupid, terrified look upon me, and then without a word

turned his nose again to the ground. An orderly that was with me at the time, told me a few moments later, that a shot struck the stone, smashing it in a thousand fragments, but did not touch the man, though his head was not six inches from the stone. [6]

Poker Face

At the Battle of Fredericksburg, Union Brevet Major General William Farrar Smith witnessed perhaps one of the few laughable incidents caused by a round shot:

> While riding along behind a regiment lying with their faces to the ground, a round shot struck the knapsack of a soldier, and cutting it open, sent a cloud of under-clothes into the air, and high above them floated a

A typical mode of entertainment for both Union and Confederate soldiers was card playing.

scattered pack of cards. The soldier, hearing the shouts of laughter, turned over to see what was the matter, and when he saw the mishap which had befallen him made a feeble effort to join in the laugh.[7]

Hooker's Luck

At the Battle of Chancellorsville, Union Major General Joseph Hooker had two near misses on the same day with Confederate round shot. The first occurred while he was standing on the porch of the Chancellor Mansion. On Sunday morning, May 3, Hooker stood on a step on the porch of the mansion. The battle was raging as Confederate artillery was pounding the area around the mansion. Suddenly, a solid shot hit the pillar closest to the general. Half the shattered column struck Hooker on the right side. He was quickly made senseless and bruised, but unharmed otherwise. Upon his urging, Hooker was lifted upon a horse and rode a short distance to the rear.

While riding, the pain in his right side became so intense that he was forced to lie down on a blanket. After a short rest and some brandy, the general was once again able to ride. Hardly was Hooker mounted, when another solid shot struck the blanket directly in the center where the general had been only moments before. In this way, Joseph Hooker avoided being instantly killed by two cannon balls within minutes of each other.[8]

A Race for the Courthouse

During the spring of 1864, the Union Army of the Potomac began its last drive to Richmond. Under the newly appointed lieutenant general, Ulysses Grant, the huge army crossed the Rapidan River and entered the Wilderness. In the tangle of trees and thickets it met its longtime rival, the Army of Northern Virginia.

After two days of fighting to a stalemate, Grant decided to move his army. Two options were open: retreat to Fredericksburg, or sidestep his opponent and move south. For Grant retreat would not work, as he intended "to fight it out all summer" and destroy the Confederate army with his vast materials and men. Therefore, the Army of the Potomac would pull out of the tangle of the Wilderness and move south-east to the little village of Spotsylvania Courthouse.[9] If successful, the Union army would be 12 miles closer to its objective of Richmond. More importantly it would place Grant between the Confederate army and the capital it was committed to defend. Lee would be forced to attack, this time on Grant's terms.

The Chancellor Mansion as seen during the Battle of Chancellorsville.

Courtesy *Battles and Leaders of the Civil War*

According to Brigadier General John Gordon, the thought of Grant moving to Spotsylvania Courthouse occurred to Lee during the afternoon of May 7. Lee reportedly told Gordon that "General Grant is not going to retreat. He will move his army to Spottsylvania [Spotsylvania]."[10] When Gordon inquired whether Lee had special knowledge of such a move, Lee replied, "Not at all . . . Spottsylvania [Spotsylvania] is now General Grant's best strategic point. I am so sure of his next move that I have already made arrangements to march by the shortest practicable route, that we may meet him there."[11]

The shortest route was a crude road cut through the Wilderness by Brigadier General William Pendleton, Lee's chief of artillery. This road extended from the Confederate left flank to the Catharpin Road. It was designed to save the Rebel army valuable time and distance should they need to move in that direction.[12] Lee ordered Major General Richard Anderson to march to Spotsylvania Courthouse by way of the path that Pendleton had cut. Ordered to start south at 3 A.M. on May 8, Anderson decided to start out at 11 P.M. the night before to allow his men some rest time along the way. As the gray column weaved its way along the path, the forest was burning, leaving no place to stop for rest. This forced Anderson to keep moving until dawn. Only then a suitable place was found for the men to rest for an hour.[13]

The first Union troops to move south were those of Major General Gouverneur Warren's V Corps. Starting out at 9 P.M., the V Corps moved along the Brock Road and sought to take possession of Spotsylvania Courthouse before the Confederate army knew of their position. Immediately the V Corps ran into trouble when their progress was slowed due

Union troops march out of the burning Wilderness, headed toward Spotsylvania.

Courtesy *Battles and Leaders of the Civil War*

to the provost guard that was escorting Major General George Meade. After the cavalry escort allowed the corps through, they were slowed further by Confederate cavalry whose mission was to do just that, slow any Union advances.[14]

The first force to reach the courthouse was Union cavalry, which had worked its way behind the Confederate army, all the while dueling with their gray counterparts. Their position was quickly taken from them when Anderson's lead elements of the Confederate I Corps arrived to take possession of Spotsylvania Courthouse.[15] Minutes later Warren's V Corps appeared on the Brock Road. The Confederates had won the race only because there was no place to rest along the fire-engulfed Wilderness road.

The Good Book

Captain Eli Daugherty of the 93rd Pennsylvania Infantry, Company K, had a close call at the Battle of Fair Oaks,

Virginia, on May 31, 1862, when a minie ball struck his heart. Fortunately, the force of the ball was broken by a gold watch and then stopped by a Bible the captain had been carrying. The following is an article recorded in the June 3, 1862, edition of the *Philadelphia Evening Bulletin*:

> In the battle Saturday [May 31, 1862], a Minie ball struck him just in the heart, or rather in the clothes over his heart. It went through his coat, vest and shirt. It smashed a gold watch (which he had bought for his sister) all to pieces. The ball then went into a Bible and dug its way through the lid and about six hundred pages. At the beginning of the 4th chapter, 2nd Timothy, it went out of the bible and inflicted a slight wound in his breast. It left its last mark on that chapter.
>
> The watch Capt. Daugherty showed us is in fragments. The Bible is so disfigured that it will only be valuable as a relic. It was given to the Captain by a lady, and his wearing it next to his heart is undoubtedly the cause of that organ continuing to beat today.[16]

On Target

One of the most remarkable strokes of luck occurred during the beginning of General William Sherman's Atlanta Campaign in May 1864. At the Battle of Rocky Face Hill, the 125th Ohio, or what is commonly known as Opdycke's Tigers, was on the firing line.

A member of the 125th pulled up his rifle to take aim. As he steadied the weapon, he felt a sharp jolt to the rifle, causing him to drop it to the ground. Upon inspection it was determined that a Rebel minie ball had entered the barrel precisely at a point to knock the gun out of the man's hands. Had this gentleman been even slightly unsteady while taking aim it is quite possible that he would have quickly joined his rifle in falling to the ground.[17]

A Good Place for a Watch

On August 5, 1864, Union Rear Admiral David Farragut entered Mobile Bay with 19 ships. His purpose was to close the important Southern port and capture the city of Mobile, Alabama. The bay was defended by numerous batteries, including Fort Morgan. Also, several Confederate gunboats helped to strengthen the bay's defenses, among them the ram CSS *Tennessee*, considered the strongest and most powerful ironclad afloat.[18]

The fighting in the bay was intense. Confederate missiles poured into the Union ships as they traveled past Fort Morgan. Ship decks quickly became slippery with blood. Dead crew members were placed in a long row on the port side while the wounded were taken below deck to be attended. One poor crewman had both legs severed by a solid shot. As he threw up his arms, another ball took them away also. Shells struck the bulwarks, destroying the lives of gunners by the tens in one shot.[19]

The U.S. steam sloop *Oneida* was ordered last in the line of vessels to pass the Confederate fortress. The crew of the *Oneida* watched and waited their turn in line as the forward ships passed the defenses of Fort Morgan. At about 7:45 in the morning she was positioned near enough to open an entire starboard broadside on the fort. The Confederate defenders were not shy in their response. Soon after Rebel batteries opened on the *Oneida*, a VII-inch rifle shell burst through the chain armor at the *Oneida*'s waterline and exploded near the starboard boiler. The carnage was terrible as crewmen nearby were either killed outright by the explosion or scalded by escaping steam. At about the same time, another VII-inch rifle shell exploded in the cabin, also entering at the waterline.

By that time, the Confederate ironclad *Tennessee* approached the already badly damaged *Oneida*. Gunners on the *Oneida* were ordered to increase powder charges and switch to solid shot. The ironclad passed alongside at not more than two hundred yards' distance. As the *Tennessee* closed on the *Oneida*, she fired her guns. Fortunately for the *Oneida*, the primers failed to explode the powder. Three times the ironclad attempted to discharge her cannons into the wounded

The Battle of Mobile Bay. The ironclad CSS *Tennessee* is pictured in the center.

Courtesy *Battles and Leaders of the Civil War*

Union sloop.[20] In the course of this action only one shell was fired. Its target was an XI-inch gun, commanded by Quartermaster James Sheridan. The shell first struck a marine, killing him instantly, and proceeded to hit the gun, sending a shower of splinters through the air. Sheridan was hit in the chest near the heart but not killed. Wounded and bleeding he stayed at the gun, firing two more rounds before the cannon became inoperable.

Sheridan examined his wound, and found that he was one of the lucky ones. When the shell hit the marine, it tore a brass button from the man's hat. The button flew into Sheridan's chest, where it struck his watch. Oddly enough, the usual place for the timepiece was to wear it on the lower right side, but Sheridan preferred to carry it in his left shirt pocket.[21]

Chapter Eight

Civil War Medicine

Alternative Medicine

Civil War battles were ghastly affairs in which men were ripped, shredded, and blown apart. For the dead, the nightmare was over. For the wounded, however, what lay ahead was many times worse than the preceding battle. With the opening shots, wounded would begin to wander to the rear. As battles progressed, the number of ravaged bodies in the rear grew. Men wandered or crawled about, bleeding from stumps that had been arms, or dragging legs that had forever ceased to walk. Their wounds were wrapped with crude bandages made from their uniforms, and rifles that were used in battle just minutes before served as crutches.

At the aid station, many of the wounded waited hours or even days to be treated by doctors who were usually overwhelmed with patients. During this wait they may have been forced to lie on a bare floor or the ground. A few lucky wounded, if there could be such a thing, might have found a real bed or church pew to use as a resting place. At times, the wounded men were exposed to the elements. The hot sun beat down, unmercifully burning the skin. During the winter, bitter cold added even more pain and suffering. Rain washed away the blood and gore of the battlefield, while soaking the wounded and adding to their misery.

If these environmental conditions weren't bad enough, the hospital or aid station could be just as horrible. Sanitation essentially did not exist—surgical procedures were commonly performed with dirty instruments that were merely wiped clean of blood and tissue on a surgeon's apron. When instruments were washed, a communal basin was generally used, the water tinted red from a dozen previous washings. Surgeons would also use hands that were unwashed and not disinfected to probe wounds and perform their work. One surgeon wrote:

> We operated in old blood-stained and often pus-stained coats, the veteran of a hundred fights. We operated with clean hands in the social sense, but they were not disinfected hands. . . . We used not disinfected instruments from not disinfected plush-lined cases, and still worse used marine sponges which had been used in prior pus cases and had been only washed in tap water. If a sponge or an instrument fell on the floor, it was washed and squeezed in a basin of tap water and used as if it were clean.[1]

Another grim picture of field surgery is painted by Major General Carl Schurz, who commanded the Third Division of the XI Corps at Gettysburg. After that great battle Schurz visited the wounded of his command at various field hospitals and observed

> . . . the surgeons, their sleeves rolled up to the elbows, their bare arms as well as their linen aprons smeared with blood, their knives not seldom held between their

A Union field hospital.

Courtesy *Battles and Leaders of the Civil War*

teeth, while they were helping a patient on or off the table, or had their hands otherwise occupied; around them pools of blood and amputated arms and legs in heaps, sometimes more than man-high. Antiseptic methods were still unknown at that time. As a wounded man was lifted on the table, often shrieking with pain as the attendants handled him, the surgeon quickly examined the wound and resolved upon cutting off the injured limb. Some ether was administered and the body put in position in a moment. The surgeon snatched the knife from between his teeth, where it had been while his hands were busy, wiped it rapidly once or twice across his blood-stained apron, and the cutting began. The operation accomplished, the surgeon would look around with a deep sigh, and then—"NEXT!"[2]

Civil War-era doctors also generally accepted the occurrence of pus to be a normal trait of the healing process. Pus was thought to be formed from dead tissue which lined the wound and was simply being expelled by the body. Charles Johnson, a Union soldier assigned to hospital duty in the western theater, wrote in his recount of the war that "so-called laudable pus was welcomed by those in charge as an indication that the patient had reached one of the mile-posts that had to be passed on his road to recovery."[3]

These crude medical techniques were not due to the lack of concern for the wounded but the lack of medical knowledge. For instance, antiseptics such as carbolic acid were used, but more often than not, were applied too late to benefit the patient. Not until 1865 did British surgeon Baron Joseph Lister discover that germs could be transferred from a hand or surgical instrument to another person, causing infection and the formation of pus. However, for the Civil War soldier this discovery was too late.[4]

Hard-Headed

Private George Sinsel of the 8th New York Heavy Artillery was struck in the head by a minie ball during a charge on the Confederate lines at Petersburg on June 16, 1864. The projectile broke his skull and then split in two. Part of the ball continued on its trajectory, while the other half imbedded itself under the head bone. After being hit, Private Sinsel lay on the battlefield for three days before coming to his senses. On the third day he finally wandered into a Union field hospital where surgeons extracted a number of bone fragments from his skull. Sinsel was eventually transferred to St. Mary's Hospital in Rochester, New York, where another surgery was performed to remove the remaining half of the Confederate ball from under his cranium.[5]

Private Sinsel received a disability discharge on February 25, 1865.[6] In time, he fully recovered from this remarkable injury that should have killed him. The only reminder of the incident was a hole in his head large enough to hold a walnut.[7]

Hard to Swallow

Lieutenant Thomas O'Brien of the 88th New York, a part of the famed Irish Brigade, was wounded while assaulting Marye's Heights during the Battle of Fredericksburg. A minie ball entered his neck and exited near the jugular vein. Even though not an uncommon injury, its effect was a bit odd. Soon after, when Lieutenant O'Brien tried to eat a piece of gingerbread, part of the bread came out through the hole in his neck.[8]

Spitting Bullets

During the Battle of Chancellorsville, Private Jacob Dunkle of Company D, 148th Pennsylvania Infantry, was wounded. He received a minie ball in the eye, as well as the arm and leg. Taken to a surgeon, the doctor washed the eye out but did not probe for the ball.

For years after the incident, Dunkle had frequent pain in his eye and constantly endured tearing. In early November 1894 he suffered a severe coughing spell. As he coughed, friends nearby noticed an object falling from his mouth. Upon inspection, they found the minie ball that thirty odd years earlier had entered Dunkle's eye. Apparently the piece of lead had worked its way to the back of his mouth where the force of the cough finally expelled it from his body.[9]

Cheating Death, Four Times Over

In some cases, surviving a wound was nothing short of a miracle. This was the case with Private John W. Vance of Company B, 72nd Indiana Mounted Infantry. On April 3, 1863, Vance and two others in his company, Privates Elma Wright and William Montgomery, were serving as pickets on a small by-road just off a main highway near Taylorville, Tennessee. Without warning, Rebel cavalry came down the highway at a full gallop with the intention of cutting the three Union men off from the rest of their company. Wright, being the advanced picket, was able to flee by burying his heels into his horse's flanks. Unfortunately, in his flight, the animal's head struck a tree and the horse fell dead. Wright was thrown from the mount some twenty feet. Landing upright, he continued to run, hurling over a fence, as his comrades, coming to his aid, had a hearty laugh at the scene.[10]

For Vance and Montgomery the outcome was much different. Unable to effect an escape, they were taken prisoners. It was near sundown as their captors, a Rebel captain and three privates, marched the two men eight miles to the town of Lebanon. Here the prisoners were kept for the night to await their fate. In an affidavit for his pension Vance described the horror he was forced to experience the next day at the hands of his captors:

> I was Tied to A Tree with a Leather Halter—This was about 11' o ck A M on the 4th of April 1863—The day after My Capture—The Captain of the Rebels after I was Tied to the Tree—Stepped off Some 7 or 10 feet & fired at me with a Colt Revolver—He fired Three Shots—Two of them went in to the Right—check

[cheek] & come out at the left cheeck [cheek] The other
Shot went in to the Right Side of My neck & was taken
out under my Left Jaw—I was then untied & Fell to
the ground another Shot was fired below my left Ear &
come out my left Eye—My Companion who was prisoner with me was Tied as I was & Shot dead.[11]

Miraculously, Vance was conscious throughout the whole
ordeal. The *History of the Seventy-Second Regiment* records that
Vance was aware of what was happening and controlled his
muscles in an effort to appear dead when he was untied from
the tree. The story goes on to state that Vance even felt the
dirt hit his face when the fourth ball impacted the ground
below his head.

Private Vance waited until he was sure his would-be kill-
ers were gone until attempting to move. By now his head lay
in a pool of blood. He tried to raise it, succeeding only after
much effort. Slowly he cleaned the mud and blood from his
face so he could look around. There by his side lay Montgomery, his lifeless body face down in the dirt, where it had
fallen.

Deciding he had no time to waste, and unable to defend himself, Vance crawled off the road to wait until the
loss of blood would cause his death. Soon a Negro wandered by and Vance decided to take a chance and attract his
attention. This gamble paid off as the wounded soldier found
himself in caring hands. His caretaker took him to the
Murfreesboro Pike and turned him over to the safety of
Union cavalry.

John Vance defied all odds and recovered from the four
gunshot wounds to his head. He was discharged from the

army on June 9, 1863, and eventually served two terms as Recorder of Tippecanoe County, Indiana.[12]

Ringing His Hand

In 1902, James M. Denn moved into the Soldiers' Home in Washington, D.C. He took with him the usual essentials, as well as a few precious mementos from the past, one of which was a minie ball from his days as a corporal in Company E, 95th Pennsylvania Infantry. It is not uncommon for a soldier to carry such an artifact, but the way Denn carried it was somewhat unusual.

During May 1864 Corporal Denn found himself in the midst of the fighting at Spotsylvania Courthouse. He was hit in the hand by a minie ball that remained lodged there. Denn found his way to Fredericksburg, where the wounded, shattered hand was dressed without removing the ball. Having a useless hand, he was given a surgeon's certificate and discharged from the service on December 28.[13]

Eventually a cyst grew around the minie ball, trapping it for 38 years. For Corporal Denn it was a constant reminder of his service to the Union. However, he also discovered a little fun in having such a novelty at his fingertips. When a young person visited the home, Denn would summon the youngster to his side. He would then proceed to shake the crippled hand next to the child's ear. The ball inside the cyst would rattle, making the youngster's eyes grow wide at such an odd noise coming from a human hand. Quite possibly one has to wonder who got more pleasure from such an attraction, the listener or the shaker.

The oddity of Denn's rattling hand did not last long while in the Soldiers' Home. When Dr. Louis A. LaGarde, a surgeon, discovered the abnormality, he immediately went about correcting it. Thus Private Denn's hand still remained crippled, but his unique trick was surgically removed during what has been considered to be the last surgical operation of the Civil War.[14]

The Flesh Eaters

During the Civil War, like every war in history, the practice of medicine was altered to suit the situation. Surgeries were performed under difficult, and many times unusual, circumstances. Sometimes necessity dictated that unorthodox or even disgusting methods be used.

One such unorthodox medical method adopted during the war was the use of maggots to aid the healing process. This concept was stumbled upon by Confederate surgeons operating in a Union prison camp at Chattanooga, Tennessee. Having limited supplies to bind wounds, the surgeons were forced to leave some open to the air. Flies were soon attracted, laying eggs in the open flesh. Oddly enough, these wounds healed faster and better than ones that remained wrapped. The maggots fed on the dead tissue of the wound, aiding the healing process. The results prompted Confederate surgeons to actually invite infestations of maggots into open wounds thereafter.[15]

Do-It-Yourself Surgery

The following is an incident related by Colonel Thomas F. Berry, who served in the cavalry commands of Brigadier General John Morgan and Lieutenant General Nathan Bedford Forrest. Colonel Berry was wounded in the bowel, which during the Civil War, was considered to be fatal.

Because of this attitude, the surgeon in the care of the colonel refused to operate and remove the ball. Colonel Berry's recollections show what determination and a strong will to live can accomplish when put to the test:

It was now a month since I had been wounded. The surgeon in charge told me the bullet could not be taken out and that he would not attempt it.

I had been in practice four years with my preceptor, who was a fine surgeon. I had assisted the surgeons often when crowded with work. From day to day I called my case to the notice of the surgeon. He still flatly refused to do the work for me. I now made up my mind to do it myself, with the assistance of a young widow nurse, who was in the hospital. She had lost her husband in the first battle of Bull Run and thereupon had become a nurse for wounded and sick soldiers. I told her my plan and told her, too, that I was dying by inches every day. I asked her if she would bring me the necessary instruments, while the surgeon was gone to his dinner. She said, "Yes, and I will help you, too." I told her to get some hot water, some carbolic acid, two pairs of scissors, one curved pair, a sharp knife, a blunt curved hook. She had all these ready when the doctor started to dinner. I asked her to bring me a bullet, a Minie ball. I got busy at once. The nurse also brought me six surgeon's needles threaded with cat-gut sutures. I placed the bullet between my teeth to bite on while doing this work, for I knew it would hurt badly.

I took up the blunt, curved hook and slowly introduced it into the wound by a slight rotary, oscillating movement from side to side. I rested for a short time, for it was very painful. I pressed further in until I felt that I had gotten the hook over the bowel. I slowly drew the bowel toward the opening, which had sloughed considerably, and left a large hole in my side. The cut in the bowel could be plainly seen. I now placed a roll of bandages in the loop of the bowel between it and my side, to keep the bowel from slipping back into the cavity. Then I took the curved scissors, snipped off the sloughing, ragged edges to freshen them. I was gritting my teeth upon the bullet. Cold perspiration was pouring off my face and body. I must not and could not stop now.

There was a horrid fascination about it. I was suffering torture. I held my breath.

[When the bullet was out] the widow handed me the curved, threaded needles; I dreaded these more than the cutting, but with a renewed determination, I placed six stitches in my bowel; I then tightened these alternately, so as to have the fresh edges fit closely without puckering. Having drawn up tightly, I took sponges and moistened them in hot water and bathed the bowel, removing all the blood clots. I took a large syringe and washed out the cavity thoroughly. After cleansing the gut wound I placed eight stitches in the outside wound.

The operation was finished. The cold perspiration was standing in great beads upon my face and body. I was frozen almost to death. The work finished, I looked up into the face of this heroic, beautiful woman. Both of us fell in a dead faint across the cot.

Colonel Berry recovered from his near fatal wound. Ironically, one of the circumstances he attributed to his successful surgery and recovery was the fact that he had not eaten for five days with the exception of a little parched corn. Had he been well fed, Berry felt he would have definitely died from the wound.[16]

Second Opinion

Another story of a surgical miracle is told by Dr. Hunter McGuire, chief surgeon on the staff of General Thomas "Stonewall" Jackson:

> After one of the battles in the valley of Virginia I was riding along a dusty road one hot day when I saw a Confederate officer lying upon the ground desperately wounded. Upon an examination I discovered that he had received a wound in the abdomen. His intestines were protruding several inches, and covered with dust. I expressed my regret at being unable to do anything for the sufferer. He was in good spirits, and replied: "Two or three other doctors have said the same thing. What I want is for some one to do something for me."
>
> Although the case appeared a hopeless one, I procured a tub of water and washed the wound, then handed him a mirror and in it he saw reflected his own liver. Upon an examination, I discovered that the walls of the stomach had not been injured. The wound sewed up and the officer rapidly recovered. The case is one of the most remarkable ones that have ever come to the knowledge of the medical profession.[17]

Rat Surgeons

Some of the most remarkable surgeries during the war were not performed by surgeons at all, in fact they were not even done by people. Phoebe Yates Pember, a Southern nurse in Richmond, relates that rats "ate all the poultices applied during the night to the sick, and dragged away the pads stuffed with bran from under the arms and legs of the wounded."[18]

As undesirable as it sounds to have rats in, of all places, a hospital, Pember does tell a story where a rat performed a surgical operation:

> A Virginian had been wounded in the very center of the instep of his left foot. The hole made was large, and the wound sloughed fearfully around a great lump of proud flesh which had formed in the center like an island. The surgeons feared to remove this mass, as it might be connected with the nerves of the foot, and lock-jaw might ensue. Poor Patterson would sit on his bed all day gazing at his lame foot and bathing it with a rueful face, which had brightened amazingly one morning when I paid him a visit. He exhibited it with great glee, the little island gone, and a deep hollow left, but the wound washed clean and looking healthy. Some skillful rat surgeon had done him this good service while in the search for luxuries, and he only knew that on awaking in the morning he found the operation performed.[19]

Even though he was afterwards grateful for the service performed by the rat surgeon, who knows how he would have felt if interrupted in his slumber during this unusual surgery? Another incidence of an operation performed by a rat is recorded in the *Petersburg Express*:

This patient was suffering from the effects of a fracture of the frontal bone of the skull a piece of which projected outwards to some length; and the healing of the fleshy parts depended upon its removal. The bone was so firmly fixed, however as, in the opinion of the surgeon, would cause unnecessary pain in its forcible removal; and such remedies were applied as would assist nature in eventually ejecting it. A soothing poultice was placed upon the part a night or two ago, a hole being made through the application for the insertion of the projecting bone. The patient was soon asleep in his bed, but during the night was aroused by the sting of pain, and awoke, to discover a rat making off with the piece of bone in his mouth. He struck at it and hit the rat, but did not hurt him. The rat had probably been drawn to the bed of the soldier by the scent of the poultice, which was pleasant to his olfactories; but on reaching it, his keen appetite, no doubt, caused him to relish, in a large degree, the juicy bone so convenient to his teeth. He therefore seized, and drew it from its position, and was made to scamper off by the patient, whom he had aroused with pain. It was a skillful operation, quickly performed, and will result beneficiary to the invalid.[20]

Chapter Nine

Tempting Fate

A Fine-Looking Corpse

During August 1, 1862, the Second Battle of Bull Run was fought to a stalemate. The next day Union reinforcements arrived on the field to bolster the Federal effort. One of these regiments was the 5th New York, which took up position on the extreme left of the Union battle line. The 5th New York Infantry was also known as Duryée's Zouaves in honor of Abram Duryée, a wealthy New York merchant who recruited the regiment. Their uniform reflected the style of the French Foreign Legion, consisting of a blue jacket with red braid, white leggings, and topped by a tasseled red fez.[1] However, the most conspicuous part was the red baggy pants that gave them their nickname of the "red-legged devils."[2]

Earlier that morning an incident took place that at the time was brushed off as mere humor, but would become more prophetic. During the march to the Bull Run battlefield the regiment came to rest at a stream. As the men cleaned off the dirt from the march and relaxed on the banks of the cool water, Captain George Hager of Company F approached his men and asked an odd question, "Boys, how do I look?"

"You look nobby," said one.

"You look bully," said another.

"Well," replied the captain, "don't you think I'd make a fine-looking corpse?"[3]

An odd question for a man who stood a great chance of soon going into battle.

The regiment resumed its march and finally arrived at its destination on the far left of the Union line. The position the 5th New York held remained fairly quiet for most of the day with the exception of an occasional stray bullet that would harmlessly hit the ground. The stray balls that did strike near the New Yorkers were somewhat of a puzzlement to the men as no Confederates could be seen. It was off to the right the battle raged with intensity as wave after wave of Union troops hammered the Confederate defensive works along an old railroad bed.

Suddenly a body of men from the 10th New York, stationed on the left of the 5th, rushed back through the woods.[4] The demoralized men began breaking through the lines of the 5th New York in a rush to flee the scene. As they ran, they "cried out that the enemy had come out of the ground, as it were, and were coming on in heavy force, and were right on top of them and on the flank."[5] Regimental commander of the 5th New York, Colonel Gouverneur Warren, ordered his men to change position to meet the attack. In the confusion the front wave of the Confederate attack, led by the Texas Brigade, came into view. Alfred Davenport reported that "The balls began to fly like hail from the woods, and the Texans were yelling like fiends; their fire directly increasing into one unceasing rattle, the air full of deadly missiles."[6]

Still the 5th New York held its fire as much as possible to allow the men of the 10th New York to pass through their lines. The Rebel assault poured out from the trees toward the waiting New Yorkers. Davenport further writes that "All along the line the fire was murderous; the enemy were on the front and flanks, and were pouring in a terrible cross fire on the men, and were endeavoring to surround and take prisoners the remnant of the regiment."[7]

With Rebels closing in, the 5th finally broke for the rear, eventually reaching the safety of the Henry House Hill.[8] In

The uniform of the 5th New York Volunteers (Duryée's Zouaves).

Courtesy *Battles and Leaders of the Civil War*

less than 15 minutes the 5th had sustained enormous casualties. Of the 490 men engaged in the fight 297 were either killed, wounded, or captured, the highest casualty rate for that period of time of any Union regiment in the war.[9] Captain George Hager, the same man who so proudly inquired whether he would make a fine-looking corpse, received his answer.[10]

An Eternal Furlough

Major General Stephen Dodson Ramseur sat on a bluff watching his Confederate division move into position near Cedar Creek, Virginia. Below him slept the Federal army, unaware of the attack that was soon to awaken them. It was just past midnight, October 19, 1864.

Stephen Dodson Ramseur was a rising star in the Confederate army. He graduated from West Point in 1860, and less than a year later resigned his commission to throw his lot in with the Confederacy. At Malvern Hill, during the end of the Seven Days' Battle, he received his first wound for the Southern cause. Then, during the Battle of Chancellorsville, he was wounded a second time. Ramseur recovered from these injuries to lead his troops in defending the Bloody Angle during the Battle of Spotsylvania. In the process he received his third wound of the war. For his service the 27-year-old Ramseur was promoted to the rank of major general, the youngest officer of such rank in the Southern military.[11]

As Ramseur sat, his thoughts drifted home to North Carolina, where that last October he had wed Ellen Richmond. For weeks he had been yearning to go home on furlough and visit his young bride. The prospect for a visit was greatly diminished due to the Confederate defeats in the Shenandoah Valley at Winchester and Fisher's Hill. However, recently, his desire for a furlough was greatly enhanced.[12]

Three days previous he had received word from the signal corps of a special message. It read, ". . .The crisis is over and all is well."[13] A mysterious message, but for Ramseur its meaning was a blessing. He was a father. However, the telegraph failed to say whether the baby was a girl or a boy. After receiving the news of the birth of his child, Ramseur sent for Brigadier General Bryan Grimes to tell him the good news. Ironically, after Grimes left Ramseur's headquarters, he was informed that his wife had also given birth. Ramseur wrote his wife:

> I rec'd last night through the Signal Corps, the tele-
> gram. It has relieved me of the greatest anxiety of my
> life. I hope that my darling precious wife & our darling
> babe too are well. . . . I cannot express my feelings. . . .
> I don't know how I can bear the separation from you
> much longer. . . . I must see you & be with you & our
> little Darling & The telegram did not state whether we
> have a son or a daughter! . . .[14]

The appointed hour for the attack finally arrived.
Ramseur turned to his corps commander, Major General John
Gordon, and saluted, saying, "Well, General, I shall get my
furlough to-day."[15] Gordon did not know what Ramseur
was referring to and did not ask an explanation. The time
for conversation was over
and the bloody work of
the day was about to
commence. The young
major general turned and
rode to his division.

At approximately 5
A.M. the attack on the
Union position at Cedar
Creek began. Confederate
troops appeared out of the
foggy morning air like
ghosts in the night to
gobble up the Union
picket line. Within min-
utes the Confederates had
entered the sleeping Fed-
eral camp. Resistance was

**Major General
Stephen Dodson Ramseur.**
Courtesy *Battles and Leaders of the Civil War*

slim. Blue-clad troopers attempted to gather themselves. But many were still asleep in their tents. Those who had risen early were only able to run for their lives.[16]

After several hours of fighting, Union Major General Philip Sheridan arrived on the field from Winchester, where he had stayed the previous night. Sheridan quickly stopped the Union rout and planned a counterattack. By 4 P.M. he was ready and the Union line went forward. Confederate troops put up a gallant fight, but could not hold back the fury of the Union advance.

Ramseur, already wounded, fought to hold what was left of his division's position as panicked Rebels fled to the rear. The fighting was fierce. Ramseur had two horses killed under him and was preparing to mount a third when a bullet ripped through his right side, penetrating both lungs. The Confederate line collapsed, with defeated Rebels fleeing back across Cedar Creek. What had earlier in the day been a Confederate victory was now not only a defeat but disaster.

The bleeding Ramseur was quickly placed in an ambulance and started for the rear. A Union surgeon, by the name of Isaac Knight, captured in the first onslaught of the morning attack, was pressed into service for the wounded major general. Not far into the retreat, with Union cavalry bearing down, Ramseur's staff decided not to press their luck, which was wearing very thin. Looking around, they spied the surgeon Knight, and surrendered the ambulance to him. Having been a prisoner just moments before, Knight then found himself the captor of a Confederate major general and his staff. The ambulance was directed to the Belle Grove Mansion. Ramseur was taken inside and laid in the front room, which the owner used as a library.[17] Being made as comfortable as possible, Ramseur struggled for breath, trying to fight off man's worst enemy, death itself.

With the battle over, old friends from Ramseur's not-so-long-ago West Point days were able to visit the dying general. Major General George Custer, Captain Henry DuPont, and Brigadier General Wesley Merritt entered the room. The Union officers were flush with victory, but now the reality of the cruel war hit home as they tried to comfort their dying friend.

The old friends were no longer enemies on opposite sides of a war, and for a moment they reflected back to better days of friendship and camaraderie. However, reality set in as the pain grew stronger and took over the dying Ramseur's senses. On his bloodstained jacket remained the white rose he wore in honor of his newborn baby; a daughter he would never see

A postwar photograph of the Belle Grove Mansion where Major General Stephen Dodson Ramseur died following the battle of Cedar Creek.

or whose name he would never know. It was a bittersweet moment as he revealed to old friends the reason he wore the flower.[18] Wesley Merritt promised to convey his last words of affection back home to his soon-to-be-widowed bride. Then, during the early hours of October 20, fate played its ugly hand as Stephen Ramseur received his eternal furlough.[19]

A Boastful Twist

"The army will remain quiet tomorrow, 9th Instant, to give the men rest and distribute ammunition and rations."[20] This order was given by the Army of the Potomac commander, Major General George Meade, following the Battle of the Wilderness and the race to Spotsylvania Courthouse.

The day of rest merely meant that there would be no major offensives, but strategic planning would still be undertaken. The men still had to build breastworks, position guns, and guard against any Confederate attacks. For Major General John Sedgwick, commander of the Union VI Corps, this day meant surveying his lines and getting them ready for the fighting that would surely come the next day.

Sedgwick rode the length of the VI Corps front with his chief of staff, Major General Martin McMahon. The terrain around Spotsylvania Courthouse was more open and conducive to the maneuver of troops, much different than in the Wilderness from where the VI Corps had arrived the previous afternoon. Before him lay open fields that were bordered on the far side by a gently sloping ridge named Laurel Hill. The day before, Union and Confederate forces had raced from the Wilderness to occupy the ground around Laurel Hill and thus secure Spotsylvania Courthouse. If Union forces could have arrived first, they would have been positioned between

Lee and Richmond. However, it was Major General Richard
Anderson's Confederate I Corps that arrived first to occupy
the strategic position. Anderson quickly threw up breastworks
and repelled repeated Union assaults. This left the two armies
facing each other once again.

Finding time to rest, Sedgwick and McMahon took a
break from their inspection tour and sat down on several hard-
tack boxes to relax. Major General John Sedgwick, or "Uncle
John," as he was affectionately known by his troops, was born
in Cornwall Hallow, Connecticut, during the year 1813. In
1837 he graduated 24th in his class at West Point and served
in the old army for several years, rising to the rank of colonel
of the 4th Regular Cavalry. Early in the Civil War Sedgwick
earned a promotion to brigadier general, commanding the
Second Division in the II Corps. At the Battle of Antietam
he was wounded but recovered to receive command of the IX
Corps for a time until taking over the VI Corps from Major
General William Farrar Smith. It was Sedgwick who commanded the VI Corps through Fredericksburg, Gettysburg,
and the Wilderness.[21]

As the two generals relaxed, they discussed matters of
the day. However, their conversation was cut short when
Sedgwick noticed troops filing into rifle pits near a section of
artillery. Following is McMahon's rendition of Sedgwick's re-
action to this maneuver and the consequences that followed:

> . . . He (Sedgwick) was interrupted in his comments
> by observing that the troops, who during this time had
> been filing from the left into the rifle-pits, had come to
> a halt and were lying down, while the left of the line
> partly overlapped the position of the section of artil-
> lery. He stopped abruptly and said, "That is wrong.

Those troops must be moved further to the right; I don't wish them to overlap that battery." I started out to execute the order, and he rose at the same moment, and we sauntered out slowly to the gun on the right. About an hour before, I had remarked to the general, pointing to the two pieces in a half-jesting manner,

Major General John Sedgwick.
Courtesy MOLLUS-MASS at USAMHI

which he well understood, "General, do you see that section of artillery? Well, you are not to go near it to-day." He answered good-naturedly, "McMahon, I would like to know who commands this corps, you or I?" I said playfully, "Well, General, sometimes I am in doubt myself"; but added, "Seriously, General, I beg of you not to go to that angle; every officer who has shown himself there has been hit, both yesterday and to-day." He answered quietly, "Well I don't know that there is any reason for my going there." When afterward we walked out to the position indicated, this conversation had entirely escaped the memory of both.

I gave the necessary order to move the troops to the right, and as they rose to execute the movement the enemy opened a sprinkling fire, partly from sharp-shooters.

As the bullets whistled by, some of the men dodged. The general said laughingly, "What! What! Men, dodging this way for single bullets! What will you do when they open fire along the whole line? I am ashamed of you. They couldn't hit an elephant at that distance." A few seconds after, a man who had been separated from his regiment passed directly in front of the general, and at the same moment a sharp-shooter's bullet passed with a long shrill whistle very close, and the soldier, who was then just in front of the general, dodged to the ground. The general touched him gently with his foot, and said, "Why, my man, I am ashamed of you, dodging that way," and repeated the remark, "They couldn't hit an elephant at this distance." The man rose, snapped a salute, and said good-naturedly "General, I dodged a shell once, and if I hadn't, it would have taken my head off. I believe in dodging." The general laughed and replied, "All right, my man; go to your place."

For a third time the same shrill whistle, closing with a dull, heavy stroke, interrupted our talk, when, as I was about to resume, the general's face turned slowly to me, the blood spurting from his left cheek under the eye in a steady stream. He fell in my direction. . . .[22]

"Uncle John" was dead.

Not Carved in Wood, but Stone

Slowly and deliberately Sergeant Major George Polley of the 10th Massachusetts Infantry chipped away pieces of wood that once served as the top of a cracker box. Once in a while he stopped to wipe away the debris and admire his work. He would then chuckle and resume carving.

Around him excitement abounded. The veterans of the 10th had just been pulled away from the trenches of Petersburg the previous evening. The day was June 20, 1864, exactly three years since they were mustered into the army. They now passed the time waiting for the order they had waited for so long: the order to go home. However, George wasn't finished with the war. He and a few others elected not to return home. Instead, they reenlisted to see the thing through to the end. After saying goodbye, they would join the 37th Massachusetts, where George would be promoted to second lieutenant.[23]

During the last day of service the men of the 10th waited near the Jordan House, named after the family that only several days before had occupied the structure and farmed its fields. Nearby was the former Confederate Battery Number 6, which served as part of the Dimmock Line. This was a line of batteries and defensive works designed by Confederate engineer Captain Charles Dimmock. Fighting in this area on June 15 had yielded a mile-wide stretch of the Dimmock Line to the Union army, which included Batteries Number 3 through Number 11.[24]

Upon finishing his carving, George showed the board to Colonel Joseph Parsons, commander of the 10th and the man whose recommendation helped secure his promotion to second lieutenant.[25] Eventually, George gave Lieutenant Elisha Hunt Rhodes, a member of the 2nd Rhode Island, a peek at his creation. Rhodes was astonished to find that George had carved his own grave marker. On it he included his name and date of birth, but left blank his date of death. This was truly an odd endeavor for one so young. But this was war and anything could happen. Elisha Rhodes inquired whether

George was ". . . expected to be killed and he (George) said no, and that he had made his headboard only for fun."[26]

By now another scene was unfolding nearby that captured the interest of George and his colleagues. A crude scaffold had been erected on the hill in front of the Jordan House. The victim was a colored soldier by the name of William Johnson from the 23rd Regiment of United States Colored Troops. He was about to be executed, by hanging, for the crime of attempting to "outrage the person of a young lady at New-Kent Courthouse."[27]

The execution was purposely held in full view of the Confederate line in order to send a message across the way. An article in *Harper's Weekly* gave an explanation as to the purpose of this morbid sideshow: "Considerable importance was given the affair, in order that the example might be made more effective."[28] This was a possible response to articles in Southern papers berating Northern troops as savages that murder the noble sons of the South and insult their women. Also at the time a great many contrabands were coming into the Union lines. By holding such a public execution, it was hoped that others would be frightened, thereby reducing the numbers flowing into the Federal camps.[29]

Prior to time of the execution a Union battery north of the Jordan House opened fire on the defenses of Petersburg. Soon 20-pound Confederate siege guns from across the Appomattox River replied. As the shelling began, the provost marshal of the Army of the Potomac, Brigadier General Marsena Patrick, ordered the troops witnessing the execution behind the hill to avoid being exposed to the fire.

At about 9:30 in the morning Johnson was carried to the scaffold in a wagon. A chaplain prayed with the accused, who had confessed his guilt. The shelling continued, making

View of the execution of William Johnson as Union troops
look on.

The execution of William Johnson in front of Petersburg,
June 20, 1864.

the situation rather unpleasant, and formalities were soon dispensed with. General Patrick, apparently not wanting to postpone his task, quickly adjusted the rope. Bandages were placed over Johnson's eyes and the drop fell. The deed was done.[30]

The shelling also soon ceased, but its effects were evident. Lying on the ground, George Polley was breathing his last gasps of air. A friend rushed to him, but George was beyond hope, the victim of a direct hit to the abdomen from an artillery shell. It was a cruel joke with an everlasting effect.

For the men of the 10th George was special. "By gallant conduct and fearlessness he had become a favorite with the whole Regiment."[31] The next day his body was taken to City Point and there buried before the regiment embarked on a mail boat for Washington. As for George's headboard, which he had so much pleasure in carving, a search was made, but to no avail. It was determined George had cut up his creation to cook that morning's coffee.

Chapter Ten

Lincoln Lore

Reflections

During the night of Friday, April 14, 1865, a single pistol shot rang out. A president was mortally wounded and a shocked nation left to mourn. April 14, 1865, was Good Friday, a day when Christians the world over observe the crucifixion of Christ. Ironically, it was the day Abraham Lincoln, the man who led the cause to preserve a nation and free its slaves, was also murdered. Two days later, Easter Sunday, was anything but a celebration of Christ's victory over death and sin. Instead, ministers around the nation spoke of the loss of a man, a mortal man.

Over the years it has been debated whether Lincoln knew his fate and had the gift of prophecy or simply realized the determination of his enemies to avenge the South. Whether a prophet or a person with haunting thoughts is not to be debated in this context. However, some incidents took place that make a student of the Civil War wonder about Lincoln's ability to predict his fate.

One such incident occurred soon after the 1860 election, while Lincoln was still in his hometown of Springfield,

Illinois. That scene was described by Lincoln himself during an interview with a reporter:

> It was just after my election in 1860, when the news had been coming in thick and fast all day, and there had been a great 'Hurrah, boys,' so that I was well tired out, and went home to rest, throwing myself down on a lounge in my chamber. Opposite where I lay was a bureau with a swinging-glass upon it . . . and, looking in that glass, I saw myself reflected, nearly at full length; but my face, I noticed, had two separate and distinct images, the tip of the nose of one being about three inches from the tip of the other. I was a little bothered, perhaps startled, and got up and looked in the glass, but the illusion vanished. On lying down again I saw it a second time—plainer, if possible, than before; and then I noticed that one of the faces was a little paler, say five shades, than the other. I got up and the thing melted away, and I went off and, in the excitement of the hour, forgot all about it—nearly, but not quite, for the thing would once in a while come up, and give me a little pang, as though something uncomfortable had happened. When I went home I told my wife about it, and a few days after I tried the experiment again, when [with a laugh], sure enough, the thing came again; but I never succeeded in bringing the ghost back after that, though once I tried very industriously to show it to my wife, who was worried about it somewhat. She thought it was 'a sign' that I was to be elected to a second term of office, and that the paleness of one of the faces was an omen that I should not see life through the last term.[1]

Lincoln's Dream

As the war neared its end, so too it appears that Lincoln understood his fate. In a conversation with Harriet Beecher Stowe, author of *Uncle Tom's Cabin*, Lincoln revealed to her that he felt he would never see the war's end, stating, "I shall never live to see peace. This war is killing me."[2] In another interview with a reporter from the *Boston Journal* Lincoln discussed the fate of the country as well as his own fate. At the time the North was weary of war and there was some discussion of a peace movement. As the two men talked of the situation, the correspondent announced that "right must eventually triumph"; and that he personally never despaired that the result would be any less than victory for the Union cause. Lincoln replied, "neither have I, but I may never live to see it. I feel a presentiment that I shall not outlast the rebellion. When it is over, my work will be done."[3]

Perhaps the strain of the war was getting the best of the great man, or did he have other reasons for such a remark? Weeks before the fatal Good Friday Lincoln had a peculiar dream. This dream was more vivid than the two images in glass and would make the most skeptical of people ponder its meaning. One evening he described it in the presence of several guests and his wife, Mary:

> "About ten days ago," said he, "I retired very late. I had been up waiting for important dispatches from the front. I could not have been long in bed when I fell into a slumber, for I was weary. I soon began to dream. There seemed to be a death-like stillness about me. Then I heard subdued sobs, as if a number of people were weeping. I thought I left my bed and

wandered downstairs. There the silence was broken by the same pitiful sobbing, but the mourners were invisible. I went from room to room; no living person was in sight, but the same mournful sounds of distress met me as I passed along. It was light in all the rooms; every object was familiar to me; but where were all the people who were grieving as if their hearts would break? I was puzzled and alarmed. What could be the meaning of all this? Determined to find the cause of a state of things so mysterious and so shocking, I kept on until I arrived at the East Room, which I entered. There I met with a sickening surprise. Before me was a catafalque, on which rested a corpse wrapped in funeral vestments. Around it were stationed soldiers who were acting as guards; and there was a throng of people, some gazing mournfully upon the corpse, whose face was covered, others weeping pitifully. 'Who is dead in the White House?' I demanded of one of the soldiers. 'The President,' was his answer; 'he was killed by an assassin!' Then came a loud burst of grief from the crowd, which awoke me from my dream. I slept no more that night; and although it was only a dream, I have been strangely annoyed by it ever since."

"That is horrid!" said Mrs. Lincoln. "I wish you had not told it. I am glad I don't believe in dreams, or I should be in terror from this time forth."

"Well," responded Mr. Lincoln, thoughtfully, "it is only a dream, Mary. Let us not say no more about it, and try to forget it."[4]

Goodbye

The idea that he might die by the hand of an assassin was very much on the mind of Lincoln throughout the war. It is known he kept a file of death threats, in which close to eighty were collected.[5] He also stated that if someone wanted to kill him badly enough they would do it. Even so, he did not favor having a military escort because it was unbecoming the chief executive of a democracy to have such attention paid to him, plus the fact that he did not want to appear as being fearful of danger.

Many nights he walked from the White House to the War Department alone—an easy target for any would-be assassin. Even in the summer of 1862, when the First Family moved into a cottage at the Soldiers' Home outside Washington, Lincoln rode, many times, the three miles into the city alone.

One night while he was riding alone to the Soldiers' Home outside the city of Washington, a gunshot shattered the silence. Lincoln's hat lifted off his head. The president wisely made a dash for the security of the Home. Later the hat was picked up, and it was discovered that a bullet hole decorated it near the top. Lincoln quickly shrugged off the incident as an accident and hid the wounded hat from his family in order not to arouse any concern.[6]

Eventually, Lincoln did accept a military guard of cavalry and then an infantry company from the 150th Pennsylvania Bucktails. But it wasn't until the autumn of 1864 that personal body guards were assigned to walk with him and guard his person around and inside the White House.[7] One of these guards was Colonel William Crook, who, after the assassination, remembered an interesting conversation he had with Lincoln the afternoon before the president attended Ford's Theater. During the conversation Lincoln revealed to Crook that, during the previous three nights, he had dreamt of his own assassination. Crook suggested the president not attend the theater that evening. However, Lincoln replied that he could not disappoint his wife.[8]

Another incident took place on that day, that at the time was not considered to be very remarkable, but in hindsight is indeed worth reviewing. During a cabinet meeting, in which Lieutenant General Ulysses Grant was a guest, the question arose as to whether there was any news from Sherman regarding the surrender of the Army of Tennessee commanded by General Joseph Johnston. To this Grant responded, there was none. Lincoln intervened and said he felt there would be important news coming soon.

With that the president revealed a dream he had the night before. It was the same dream he had had just prior to several important military events during the past four years. He turned to Gideon Welles, secretary of the navy, and said, "It relates to your element, the water. I seemed to be in some indescribable vessel and I was moving with great rapidity toward an indefinite shore. I had this dream preceding Sumter, and Bull Run, Antietam, Gettysburg, Stone River, Vicksburg, and Wilmington." Upon hearing the mentioning of the Battle of Stone River, Grant responded that "Stone River was certainly no victory, nor can I think of any great results following it." Lincoln agreed to this suggestion but maintained the dream was usually followed by good news. The president then went on to say, "I had this strange dream again last night and we shall, judging from the past, have great news very soon. I think it must be from Sherman. My thoughts are in that direction. . . ." [9]

There was no word of surrender that day. However, Johnston did write to Sherman asking the Union general whether he would be "willing to make a temporary suspension of active operations." [10]

During the afternoon the president and Mrs. Lincoln went for a drive. It was a pleasant and well-deserved ride alone for the first couple. The president was in unusually high spirits. The pressures of the office had seemed to lighten as the war was now in the last throes of life. The two reminisced together of days long before when the burden of the presidency was not upon them. They then focused their attention

Ford's Theater, the site of President Abraham Lincoln's assassination on the night of April 14, 1865.

Courtesy MOLLUS-MASS at USAMHI

on the future that looked bright for the first time in many years. The couple spoke of returning home to Illinois and setting up a law practice when the second term of office was finished. The idea of touring the world and visiting California also came to light.

Mrs. Lincoln was delighted that her husband was in such a jovial mood. However, she couldn't help remembering the last time she witnessed such a carefree attitude in her husband. "I have seen you thus only once before. It was just before our dear Willie died."[11]

Later that night, as Lincoln left his office to enter the bedroom, he passed the guard, Crook. Stopping outside his chambers, the president turned as usual to say good night— but this time was different. The doomed man turned and said, "Good bye, Crook."[12] The next morning at 7:22 A.M. Abraham Lincoln was dead.[13]

Notes

Chapter One
Signs of the Times

Tearing the Union Apart

1. Julia Taft Bayne, *Tad Lincoln's Father* (Boston: Little Brown, and Company, 1931), 115.

Where Eagles Soar

2. *The Lycoming Gazette*, April 24, 1861.
3. Frazar Kirkland, *Reminiscences of the Blue and Gray '61–'65* (Chicago: The Preston Publishing Co., 1895), 39.
4. Ibid., 390.

The Union Shall Go On

5. Margaret Leech, *Reveille in Washington* (New York: Harper & Brother, 1941), 278, 279.
6. United States Capitol Historical Society, *We, the People: The Story of the United States Capitol* (Washington, D.C.: The United States Capitol Historical Society, 1976), 41.
7. Leech, *Reveille in Washington*, 279.
8. United States Capitol Historical Society, *We, the People*, 54.
9. Leech, *Reveille in Washington*, 279.
10. United States Capitol Historical Society, *We, the People*, 57.
11. Bayne, *Tad Lincoln's Father*, 179.

The Sword of Jackson

12. A. L. Long, *Memoirs of Robert E. Lee* (Richmond: J. M. Stoddart & Company, 1886), 258.
13. Robert Underwood Johnson and Clarence Clough Buel, eds. *Battles and Leaders of the Civil War*, 4 vols. (New York: The Century Company, 1884–1888) III, 211.

128

14. Mary Anna Jackson, *Life and Letters of General Thomas J. Jackson* (New York: Harper & Brother, 1892), 449.

15. John Bowers, *Stonewall Jackson: Portrait of a Soldier* (New York: Morrow, 1989), 349.

16. Hunter McGuire, *The Confederate Cause and Conduct in the War Between the States* (Richmond: L. H. Jenkins, 1907), 213.

Chapter Two
Predictions

A Grave Flesh Wound

1. John Gibbon, *Personal Recollections of the Civil War* (Dayton: Morningside Bookshop, 1988), 49–50.

2. Rufus R. Dawes, *Service with the Sixth Wisconsin Volunteers* (Marietta: E. R. Alderman & Sons, 1890), 60–61.

3. Ibid.

4. *The Milwaukee Telegraph*, July 27, 1895.

5. Ibid.

6. Ibid.

7. Ibid.

"Faithful Unto Death"

8. Washington Davis, *Camp-fire Chats of the Civil War* (Chicago: S. C. Miller, 1886), 289–93.

Private Scott's Anguish

9. United States War Department. *A Compilation of the Official Records of the Union and Confederate Armies*, vol. 25, chap. 37, no. 296, Report of Colonel Jacob Higgins, One hundred and twenty-fifth Pennsylvania Infantry, 756. (Cited hereafter as *O.R.* All volumes are in Series 1)

10. Regimental Committee, *History of the One Hundred Twenty-fifth Regiment Pennsylvania Volunteers 1862–1863* (Philadelphia: J. B. Lippincott Company, 1906), 191.

11. Samuel P. Bates, *History of the Pennsylvania Volunteers 1861–5*, 5 vols. (Harrisburg: B. Singerly, 1870), IV, 108–10.

12. *O.R.* Higgins, 756.

13. Bates, *Pennsylvania Volunteers*, IV, 111–26.

Mustered Out

14. Johnson and Buel, *Battles and Leaders*, IV, 568.

15. Dawes, *Service with the Sixth Wisconsin Volunteers*, 297.

16. *The Milwaukee Telegraph*, July 27, 1895.

17. Alan D. Gaff, *On Many a Bloody Field, Four Years in the Iron Brigade* (Bloomington: Indiana University Press, 1996), 377.

18. William J. K. Beaudot and Lance J. Herdegen, eds. *An Irishman in the Iron Brigade, The Civil War Memoirs of James P. Sullivan, Sergt., Company K, 6th Wisconsin Volunteers* (New York: Fordham University Press, 1993), 125.
19. Gaff, *On Many a Bloody Field*, 377.
20. Beaudot and Herdegen, *An Irishman in the Iron Brigade*, 126.

Death at Winchester

21. John B. Gordon, *Reminiscences of the Civil War* (New York: Charles Scribner's Sons, 1903), 61.
22. *O.R.,* vol. 43, chap. 55, no. 69, Report of Captain George W. Hoge, One hundred and twenty-sixth Ohio Infantry, 264.
23. Gordon, *Reminiscences*, 62.

A President Gets His Head Examined

24. Nelson Sizer and H. S. Drayton, *Heads and Faces and How to Study Them, A Manual of Phrenology and Physiognomy* (New York: Fowler & Wells Co., 1889), 7.
25. John D. Davies, *Phrenology Fad and Science: A 19th-Century American Crusade* (New Haven: Yale University Press, 1955), 6–7.
26. Sizer, *Heads and Faces*, 195.
27. Ibid., 7.
28. Ibid., 38.
29. Daniel Haskel and J. Calvin Smith, *Descriptive and Statistical Gazetteer of the United States of America* (New York: Sherman & Smith, 1843), 541.
30. J. T. Headley, *The Life of Ulysses S. Grant, General-In-Chief U.S.A.* (New York: E. B. Treat & Company, 1868), 23–24.

Straggling unto Death

31. W. C. King and W. P. Derby, comps., *Camp-Fire Sketches and Battle-Field Echoes* (Springfield, Mass.: King, Richardson & Co., 1888), 22.
32. James L. Bowen. *History of the Thirty-Seventh Regiment Massachusetts Volunteers in the Civil War of 1861–1865* (Holyoke, Mass.: Clark W. Bryan & Co., 1884), 159.
33. Ibid., 164–71.
34. W. C. King and W. P. Derby, *Camp-Fire Sketches*, 22.
35. Bowen, *History of the Thirty-Seventh Massachusetts*, 176.
36. Frank Aretas Haskell, *The Battle of Gettysburg* (Boston, 1908), 48.
37. Bowen, *History of the Thirty-Seventh Massachusetts*, 185.
38. Ibid., 186.
39. King and Derby, *Camp-Fire Sketches*, 22.
40. Ibid.

Meeting Fate in the Wilderness

41. *O.R.*, vol. 36, chap. 48, no. 128, Report of Brigadier General Lysander Cutler U.S. Army, commanding Fourth Division, 610.

42. *The Milwaukee Telegraph*, July 27, 1895.
43. Dawes, *Service with the Sixth Wisconsin Volunteers*, 259.
44. Ibid.
45. William DeLoss Love, *Wisconsin in the War of The Rebellion* (Chicago: Church and Goodman, 1866), 934.
46. Love, *Wisconsin in the War*, 934.
47. Dawes, *Service with the Sixth Wisconsin Volunteers*, 260.
48. Ibid.
49. Love, *Wisconsin in the War*, 934.
50. *The Milwaukee Telegraph*, July 27, 1895.

Chapter Three

Coincidences

Lexington, Concord, and Baltimore

1. Frederic A. Godcharles, *Pennsylvania Political, Governmental, Military and Civil* (New York: The American Historical Society, 1933), Military Vol. 364.
2. Frank Moore, ed., *The Rebellion Record: A Diary of American Events,* 12 vols. (New York: G. P. Putnam, 1862), I, 58.
3. Mary A. Hedrick, *Incidents of the Civil War During the Four Years of Its Progress* (Lowell, Mass.: Vox Populi Press, S. W. Huse & Co. 1888), 2.
4. John B. Dennis, *March of the Old 6th Massachusetts, A Paper Read before the Nebraska Commandery of the Military Order of the Loyal Legion of the United States* (Omaha, June 6, 1888), 24–25.
5. Glenn F. Williams, "Under the Despot's Heel," *America's Civil War* (May 2000), 22.
6. John W. Hanson, *Historical Sketch of the Old Sixth Massachusetts Volunteers during Its Three Campaigns of 1861, 1862, 1863, and 1864* (Boston: Lee and Shepard, 1866), 25–26.
7. *O.R.,* vol. 2, chap. 9, no. 1, Report of Colonel Edward F. Jones, Sixth Massachusetts Militia, 7.
8. Dennis, *March of the Old 6th Massachusetts*, 24.
9. Hedrick, *Incidents of the Civil War*, 42.
10. Ibid., 46.

Lived Together, Died Together

11. Philip Cheek, *History of the Sauk County Riflemen, Known as Company "A," Sixth Wisconsin Veteran Volunteer Infantry 1861–1865* (Madison: Democrat Printing Company, 1909), 217.
12. Love, *Wisconsin in the War*, 290.
13. *O.R.*, vol. 19, chap. 31, no. 25, Reports of Lieutenant Colonel Edward S. Bragg, Sixth Wisconsin Infantry, 254.
14. Johnson and Buel, *Battles and Leaders*, II, 639.
15. Cheek, *History of the Sauk County Riflemen*, 217.

16. Ibid.

In the Beginning and in the End

17. Frederick Maurice, ed., *An Aide-De-Camp of Lee: Being the Papers of Colonel Charles Marshall Sometimes Aide-De-Camp, Military Secretary, and Assistant Adjutant General on the Staff of Robert E. Lee 1862–1865* (Boston: Little, Brown, and Company, 1927), 268–69.

18. Johnson and Buel, *Battles and Leaders*, IV, 739.

19. Ibid., 743–44.

20. Burke Davis, *The Civil War: Strange and Fascinating Facts* (New York: The Fairfax Press, 1982), 21.

21. B. A. Botkin, ed., *A Civil War Treasury of Tales, Legends and Folklore* (New York: Promontory Press, 1960), 491.

Déjà Vu in the Wilderness

22. Johnson and Buel, *Battles and Leaders*, IV, 125.

23. James Longstreet, *From Manassas to Appomattox: Memoirs of the Civil War in America*, reprint (New York: Mallard Press, 1991), 561–62.

24. Ibid., 568.

25. Ibid., 563–66.

A Pleasant Surprise

26. George B. Herbert, *The Popular History of the Civil War* (New York: F. M. Lupton, 1885), 533–34.

Chapter Four
Ghosts

Love's Last Breath

1. Long, *The Civil War Day By Day*, 296.

2. *O.R.*, vol. 21, chap. 33, no. 271, Major General Lafayette McLaws, 581.

3. George H. Washburn, *A Complete Military History and Record of the 108th Regiment N.Y. Vols. From 1862 to 1894* (Rochester: E. R. Andrews, 1894), 14.

4. Kirkland, *Reminiscences of the Blue and Gray '61–'65*, 547–48.

Coming Home

5. St. Clair A. Mulholland, *The Story of the 116th Regiment Pennsylvania Volunteers in the War of the Rebellion* (Philadelphia: F. McManus, Jr. & Co., 1903), 314–16.

The Ghosts of Cedar Creek

6. Clifton Johnson, *Battleground Adventures, The Stories of Dwellers on the Scenes of Conflict in Some of the Most Notable Battles of the Civil War* (Boston: Houghton Mifflin Company, 1915), 416–22.

Chapter Five
Dreams

The Spotted Hand

1. Charles Morris, *Half Hours with American History*, 2 vols. (Philadelphia: J. B. Lippincott, 1887), II, 319–26.
2. Moore, *The Rebellion Record*, I, 7.

"Just What I Dreamed"

3. King and Derby, *Camp-Fire Sketches*, 517.
4. *O.R.*, vol. 40, chap. 63, rep. no. 126, Lieutenant Colonel George B. Damon, Tenth Vermont Infantry, First Brigade, Third Division of Operations March 25, 307.
5. King and Derby, *Camp-Fire Sketches*, 517–18.
6. G. G. Benedict, *Vermont in the Civil War*, 2 vols. (Burlington, Vt.: The Free Press Assoc., 1886, 1888), II, 331–32.
7. *O.R.* Damon, 308.
8. Benedict, *Vermont in the Civil War*, II, 332.

Nightmare of Home

9. Gordon, *Reminiscences*, 62–63.

Jenkins' Troubling Dream

10. Longstreet, *From Manassas to Appomattox*, 433.
11. James K. Swisher, *Prince of Edisto, Brigadier General Micah Jenkins C.S.A.* (Berryville, Va.: Rockbridge Publishing Company, 1996), 139–40.
12. Ibid, 140.
13. Ibid., 143.
14. Johnson and Buel, *Battles and Leaders* IV, 125.
15. *O.R.* vol. 36, chap. 48, no. 275, Report of Lieutenant General James Longstreet, C.S. Army, Commanding First Army Corps, of operations April 14–May 6.
16. Longstreet, *From Manassas to Appomattox*, 563.
17. Ibid., 563–64.
18. Swisher, *Prince of Edisto*, 147.
19. Longstreet, *From Manassas to Appomattox*, 564.
20. Swisher, *Prince of Edisto*, 147.

Chapter Six
Natural Wonders

The War Comets

1. *New York Herald*, April 16, 1861.

2. Bayne, *Tad Lincoln's Father*, 71–73.

3. George F. Chambers, *The Story of the Comets* (Oxford: Clarendon Press, 1910), 153.

4. *New York Herald*, July 4, 1861.

5. *Philadelphia Daily Evening Bulletin*, Tuesday, July 2, 1861.

6. *American Journal of Science and Arts*, vol. 82, Nov. 1861, 255.

7. David C. Knight, *Comets* (New York: Franklin Watts, 1968), 68.

8. *American Journal of Science and Arts*, 252.

9. *Philadelphia Daily Evening Bulletin*, July 3, 1861.

10. *New York Times*, July 4, 1861.

A Heavenly Army

11. Frank Moore, *The Civil War in Song and Story* (New York: P. F. Collier, 1889), 373.

A Mirage in the Clouds

12. Robert Marshall Utley, *Cavalier in Buckskin: George Armstrong Custer and the Western Military Frontier* (Norman: University of Oklahoma Press, 1988), 165.

13. D. A. Kinsley, *Favor the Bold* (New York: Holt, Rinehart and Winston, 1968), 200.

14. Utley, *Cavalier in Buckskin*, 165–67.

Providence Spring

15. *O.R.* ser. II, vol. 7, Report of Brigadier General R. H. Chilton, Inspector-General, 136.

16. W. B. Smith, *On Wheels and How I Came There* (New York: Hunt & Eaton, 1893), 225–27.

17. *O.R.* ser. II, vol. 8, Report of Surgeon Joseph Jones, 592.

18. Ibid., 596–97..

19. Smith, *On Wheels*, 227.

20. Ibid., 226.

21. John W. Urban, *My Experiences Mid Shot and Shell and in Rebel Den* (Lancaster, 1892), 501–4.

22. Ibid., 555.

23. Smith, *On Wheels*, 239.

With Charity for All

24. Leech, *Reveille in Washington*, 38.

25. Smith Stimmel, *Personal Reminiscences of Abraham Lincoln*, LeRoy A. Fladseth, ed. (Kearney, Neb.: Morris Publishing, 1997), 40.

26. E. B. Long, *The Civil War Day by Day* (New York: Doubleday and Company, 1971), 647.

27. Stimmel, *Personal Reminiscences*, 40.

28. Abraham Lincoln, *Second Inaugural Address*.
29. Stimmel, *Personal Reminiscences*, 41–42.

Chapter Seven
Dumb Luck

Hits and Misses with the Big Guns

1. Edward Anderson, *Camp Fire Stories, A Series of Sketches of the Union Army in the Southwest* (Chicago: Star Publishing Company, 1900), 192.
2. David G. Martin, *Gettysburg July 1* (Chonshohocken, Pa.: Combined Books, 1996), 185.
3. Abram P. Smith, *History of the Seventy-Sixth Regiment New York Volunteers* (Cortland, N.Y.: Truair, Smith, and Miles, 1867), 372.

No Place to Hide

4. Frank Wilkeson, *Recollections of a Private Soldier in the Army of the Potomac* (London: George Redman, 1898), 161.

Too Close for Comfort

5. Haskell, *The Battle of Gettysburg* (Boston: Wisconsin History Commission, 1908), 51.
6. Ibid., 51–52.

Poker Face

7. Johnson and Buel, *Battles and Leaders*, III, 137.

Hooker's Luck

8. Johnson and Buel, *Battles and Leaders*, III, 220–21.

A Race for the Courthouse

9. *O.R.*, vol. 36, pt. 1, chap. 48, General Ulysses Grant to Chief of Staff Major General Henry Halleck, 627.
10. Gordon, *Reminiscences*, 268–69.
11. Ibid.
12. *O.R.*, vol. 36, pt. 1, chap. 48, no. 274, Brigadier General William N. Pendleton, C.S. Army, Chief of Artillery, 1041.
13. *O.R.*, vol. 36, pt. 1, chap. 48, Diary of the First Army Corps, 1056.
14. *O.R.*, vol. 36, pt. 1, chap. 48, no. 98, Journal of Major-General Gouverneur K. Warren, U.S. Army, Commanding Fifth Corps, 540.
15. *O.R.*, Diary, First Corps, 1056.

The Good Book

16. Penrose G. Mark, *Red: White: and Blue Badge, Pennsylvania Veteran Volunteers A History of the 93rd Regiment, Known as the "Lebanon Infantry" and "One of the 300 Fighting Regiments" from September 12th, 1861 to June 27th, 1865* (The

Executive Committee of the 93rd Pennsylvania Veteran Volunteers Association), 354.

On Target

17. Rev. Nixon B. Stewart, *Dan McCook's Regiment 52nd O.V.I., A History of the Regiment, Its Campaigns and Battles from 1862 to 1865* (published by the author, 1900), 98–99.

A Good Place for a Watch

18. Johnson and Buel, *Battles and Leaders*, IV, 384.
19. Ibid., 391.
20. *Official Record of the Union and Confederate Navies in the War of the Rebellion*, ser. 1, vol. 21, 479.
21. Kirkland, *Reminiscences of the Blue and Gray,* 384.

Chapter Eight
Civil War Medicine

Alternative Medicine

1. George Worthington Adams, *Doctors in Blue: The Medical History of the Union Army in the Civil War* (New York: Henry Schuman, 1952), 125.
2. Frederic Bancroft, and William A. Dunning, eds., *The Reminiscences of Carl Schurz, With a Sketch of His Life and Public Services from 1869 to 1906* (New York: The McClure Co., 1908), 38–40.
3. Charles Beneulyn Johnson, *Muskets and Medicine, or Army Life in the Sixties* (Philadelphia: F. A. Davis Co., 1917), 129–34.
4. Adams, *Doctors in Blue*, 129.

Hard-Headed

5. King and Derby, *Camp-Fire Sketches*, 424.
6. *Annual Report of New York for the Year 1897*, 745.
7. King and Derby, *Camp-Fire Sketches*, 424.

Hard to Swallow

8. William Corby, *Memoirs of Chaplain Life* (Notre Dame: Scholastic Press, Inc., 1894), 132, 133.

Spitting Bullets

9. *Mifflinburg Telegraph*, November 16, 1894.

Cheating Death Four Times Over

10. B. F. McGee, *History of the 72nd Indiana Volunteer Infantry of the Mounted Lightning Brigade*, William R. Jewell ed. (LaFayette, Ind.: S. Vater & Co., 1882), 109–10.
11. National Archives and Records Administration, John W. Vance.

12. McGee and Jewell, *History of the 72nd Indiana*, 111.

Ringing His Hand

13. Bates, *History of the Pennsylvania Volunteers*, III, 357.

14. Frank R. Freeman, *Gangrene and Glory, Medical Care During the American Civil War* (Madison: Dickinson University Press, 1998), 229.

The Flesh Eaters

15. Adams, *Doctors in Blue*, 129.

Do-It-Yourself Surgery

16. Thomas F. Berry, *Four Years with Morgan and Forrest* (Oklahoma City: The Harlow-Ratliff Co., 1914), 253–56.

Second Opinion

17. King and Derby, *Camp-Fire Sketches*, 116.

Rat Surgeons

18. Phoebe Yates Pember, *A Southern Woman's Story* (New York: G. W. Carleton & Co., 1879), 102–3.

19. Ibid., 103.

20. Frank Moore, ed., *The Civil War in Song and Story 1860–1865* (New York: P. F. Collier, 1889), 153.

Chapter Nine
Tempting Fate

A Fine-Looking Corpse

1. John Hennessy, "At the Vortex of Hell," *Civil War Times Illustrated* (January 1986), 12.

2. Johnson, *Campfire and Battlefield*, 45.

3. Alfred Davenport, *Camp and Field Life of the Fifth New York Volunteer Infantry, Duryee Zouaves* (New York: Dick and Fitzgerald, 1879), 296.

4. Ibid., 273.

5. Davenport, *Fifth New York Volunteer Infantry*, 275–77.

6. Ibid., 275.

7. Ibid., 277.

8. Ibid.

9. Ibid., 283.

10. Ibid., 286.

An Eternal Furlough

11. Ezra J. Warner, *Generals in Gray, Lives of Confederate Commanders* (New Orleans: The Louisiana State University Press, 1959), 251–52.

12. Henry Steele Commager, *The Blue and the Gray* (Indianapolis: Bobbs-Merrill Co., 1982), 1048.

13. Gary W. Gallagher, *Stephen Dodson Ramseur: Lee's Gallant General* (Chapel Hill: The University of North Carolina Press, 1985), 155.

14. Commager, *The Blue and the Gray*, 1049.

15. Gordon, *Reminiscenses*, 64.

16. Edward J.Stackpole, *Sheridan in the Shenandoah* (Harrisburg: Stackpole Books, 1992), 298–301.

17. Stackpole, *Sheridan in the Shenandoah*, 336–37.

18. Commager, *The Blue and the Gray*, 1042.

19. Jeffery D. Wert, *From Winchester to Cedar Creek: The Shenandoah Campaign of 1864* (New York: Simon & Schuster Inc., 1987), 238.

A Boastful Twist

20. *O.R.,* vol. 36, pt. 1, chap. 48, General George Meade, Headquarters Army of the Potomac, 529.

21. Ezra J. Warner, *Generals in Blue* (Louisana State University Press, 1964), 430, 431.

22. Johnson and Buel, *Battles and Leaders,* McMahon Article, IV, 175.

Not Carved in Wood, but Stone

23. Massachusetts Adjutant General, *Massachusetts Soldiers, Sailors, and Marines,* 171.

24. Time Life, William C. Davis, ed., *Death in the Trenches: Grant at Petersburg* (Alexandria: Time Life Books, 1986), 42.

25. National Archives and Records Administration, George Polley.

26. Robert Hunt Rhodes, ed., *All for the Union: The Civil War Diary and Letters of Elisha Hunt Rhodes* (New York: Orion Books, 1985), 164.

27. *New York Times,* June 23, 1864.

28. *Harper's Weekly,* VIII, July 1864, 445.

29. Frank Rauscher, *Music on the March 1862–65 with the Army of the Potomac* (Philadelphia: William F. Fell & C., 1892), 190.

30. Noah Andrea Trudeau, *The Last Citadel: Petersburg, Virginia June 1864–April 1865* (Boston: Little Brown & Company, 1991), 61, 62.

31. Alfred S. Roe, *The Tenth Regiment Massachusetts Volunteer Infantry 1861–1864* (Springfield, Mass.: Tenth Regiment Veterans Assoc., 1909), 291.

Chapter Ten
Lincoln Lore

Reflections

1. *Harper's Monthly Magazine,* July 1865, 224, 225.

Lincoln's Dream

 2. Lloyd Lewis, *Myths after Lincoln* (New York: The Press of the Readers Club, 1941), 292.

 3. Henry J. Raymond, *The Life and Public Services of Abraham Lincoln* (New York: Derby and Miller Publishers, 1865), 727–28.

 4. Paul M. Angle, ed., *The Lincoln Reader* (New Brunswick, 1947), 521, 522.

Goodbye

 5. Jim Bishop, *The Day Lincoln Was Shot* (New York: Harpers and Brothers, 1955), 105.

 6. Anthony Cross, *Lincoln's Own Stories* (New York: Garden City Publishing Co. Inc., 1912), 130.

 7. Leech, *Reveille in Washington*, 302–3.

 8. Lewis, *Myths after Lincoln*, 297.

 9. Bishop, *The Day Lincoln Was Shot*, 126.

10. Long, *The Civil War Day by Day*, 676.

11. James Morgan, *Abraham Lincoln, the Boy and the Man* (New York: Grosset & Dunlap, 1910), 388.

12. Lewis, *Myths after Lincoln*, 297.

13. Long, *The Civil War Day by Day*, 677.

Bibliography

Books

Adams, George Worthington. *Doctors in Blue: The Medical History of the Union Army in the Civil War*. New York: Henry Schuman, 1952.

Anderson, Edward. *Camp Fire Stories, A Series of Sketches of the Union Army in the Southwest*. Chicago: Star Publishing Company, 1900.

Angle, Paul M. *The Lincoln Reader*. New Brunswick: Rutgers University Press, 1947.

Annual Report of New York for the Year 1897, 1898.

Bancroft, Frederic, and William A. Dunning, eds. *The Reminiscences of Carl Schurz, With a Sketch of His Life and Public Services from 1869–1906*. New York: The McClure Co., 1908.

Bates, Samuel P. *History of the Pennsylvania Volunteers 1861–5*. 5 vols. Harrisburg: B. Singerly, 1906.

Bayne, Julia Taft. *Tad Lincoln's Father*. Boston: Little, Brown, and Company, 1931.

Beaudot, William J. K., and Lance J. Herdegen, eds. *An Irishman in the Iron Brigade, The Civil War Memoirs of James*

P. Sullivan, Sergt., Company K, 6th Wisconsin Volunteers. New York: Fordham University Press, 1993.

Benedict, G. G. *Vermont in the Civil War: A History of the Part Taken by the Vermont Soldiers and Sailors in the War For the Union 1861–5.* 2 vols. Burlington, Vt.: The Free Press Assoc., 1886 & 1888.

Berry, Thomas F. *Four Years with Morgan and Forrest.* Oklahoma City: The Harlow-Ratliff Co., 1914.

Bishop, Jim. *The Day Lincoln Was Shot.* New York: Harper and Brothers, 1955.

Botkin, B. A., ed. *A Civil War Treasury of Tales, Legends and Folklore.* New York: Promontory Press, 1960.

Bowen, James L. *History of the Thirty-Seventh Regiment Massachusetts Volunteers in the Civil War of 1861–1865.* Holyoke, Mass.: Clark W. Bryan & Co., 1884.

Bowers, John. *Stonewall Jackson: Portrait of a Soldier.* New York: Morrow, 1989.

Chambers, George F. *The Story of the Comets.* Oxford: Clarendon Press, 1910.

Cheek, Philip. *History of the Sauk County Riflemen, Known as Company "A," Sixth Wisconsin Veteran Volunteer Infantry, 1861–1865.* Madison: Democrat Printing Company, 1909.

Commager, Henry Steele. *The Blue and the Gray.* 2 vols. Indianapolis: 1950 (Bobbs-Merrill reprint, 1982).

Corby, William. *Memoirs of Chaplain Life.* Notre Dame: Scholastic Press, Inc., 1894.

Cross, Anthony. *Lincoln's Own Stories.* New York: Garden City Publishing Co. Inc., 1912.

Davenport, Alfred. *Camp and Field Life of the Fifth New York Volunteer Infantry (Duryee Zouaves)*. New York: Dick and Fitzgerald, 1879.

Davies, John D. *Phrenology Fad and Science: A 19th-Century American Crusade*. New Haven: Yale University Press, 1955.

Davis, Burke. *The Civil War: Strange and Fascinating Facts*. New York: The Fairfax Press, 1982.

Davis, Washington. *Camp-fire Chats of the Civil War*. Chicago: S. C. Miller, 1886.

Dawes, Rufus R. *Service with the Sixth Wisconsin Volunteers*. Marietta: E. R. Alderman & Sons, 1890.

Dennis, John B. *March of the Old 6th Massachusetts, A Paper Read before the Nebraska Commandery of the Military Order of the Loyal Legion of the United States*. Omaha: June 6, 1888.

Freeman, Frank R. *Gangrene and Glory, Medical Care During the American Civil War*. Madison: Dickinson University Press, 1998.

Gaff, Alan D. *On Many a Bloody Field, Four Years in the Iron Brigade*. Bloomington: Indiana University Press, 1996.

Gallagher, Gary W. *Stephen Dodson Ramseur: Lee's Gallant General*. Chapel Hill: The University of North Carolina Press, 1985.

Gibbon, John. *Personal Recollections of the Civil War*. Dayton: Morningside Bookshop, 1988.

Godcharles, Frederic, A. *Pennsylvania Political, Governmental, Military, and Civil*. 5 vols. New York: The American Historical Society, Inc. 1933.

Gordon, John B. *Reminiscences of the Civil War*. New York: Charles Scribner's Sons, 1903.

Hanson, John W. *Historical Sketch of the Old Sixth Massachusetts Volunteers during Its Three Campaigns of 1861, 1862, 1863, and 1864.* Boston: Lee and Shepard, 1866.

Haskel, Daniel, and J. Calvin Smith. *Descriptive and Statistical Gazetteer of the United States of America.* New York: Sherman & Smith, 1843.

Haskell, Frank Aretas. *The Battle of Gettysburg.* Boston: Wisconsin History Commission, 1908.

Headley, J. T. *The Life of Ulysses S. Grant, General-in-Chief U.S.A.* New York: E. B. Treat & Company, 1868.

Hedrick, Mary A. *Incidents of the Civil War during the Four Years of Its Progress.* Lowell, Mass.: Vox Populi Press, S.W. Huse & Co. 1888.

Herbert, George B. *The Popular History of the Civil War.* New York: F. M. Lupton, 1885.

Jackson, Mary Anna. *Life and Letters of General Thomas J. Jackson.* New York: Harper and Brother, 1892.

Johnson, Charles Beneulyn. *Muskets and Medicine, or Army Life in the Sixties.* Philadelphia: F. A. Davis Co., 1917.

Johnson, Clifton. *Battleground Adventures, The Stories of Dwellers on the Scenes of Conflict in Some of the Most Notable Battles of the Civil War.* Boston: Houghton Mifflin Company, 1915.

Johnson, Robert Underwood, and Clarence Clough Buel, eds. *Battles and Leaders of the Civil War.* 4 vols. New York: The Century Company, 1884–88.

Kinsley, D. A. *Favor the Bold.* New York: Holt, Rinehart and Winston, 1968.

King W. C., and W. P. Derby, comps. *Camp-Fire Sketches and Battle-Field Echoes.* Springfield, Mass.: King, Richardson & Co., 1888.

Kirkland, Frazar. *Reminiscences of the Blue and Gray '61–'65.* Chicago: The Preston Publishing Co., 1895.

Knight, David C. *Comets.* New York: Franklin Watts, 1968.

Leech, Margaret. *Reveille in Washington.* New York: Harper & Brothers, 1941.

Lewis, Lloyd. *Myths after Lincoln.* New York: The Press of the Readers Club, 1941.

Long, A. L. *Memoirs of Robert E. Lee*, Richmond: J. M. Stoddart & Company, 1886.

Long, E. B. *The Civil War Day By Day: An Almanac 1861–1865.* New York: Doubleday and Company, 1971.

Longstreet, James. *From Manassas to Appomattox: Memoirs of the Civil War in America*, reprint. New York: Mallard Press, 1991.

Love, William DeLoss. *Wisconsin in the War of The Rebellion.* Chicago: Church and Goodman, 1866.

Mark, Penrose G. *Red: White: and Blue Badge, Pennsylvania Veteran Volunteers A History of the 93rd Regiment, Known as the "Lebanon Infantry" and "One of the 300 Fighting Regiments" from September 12th, 1861 to June 27th, 1865.* The Executive Committee of the 93rd Pennsylvania Veteran Volunteers Association, 354.

Martin, David G. *Gettysburg, July 1.* Revised ed. Conshohocken, Pa.: Combined Books, 1996.

Massachusetts Adjutant General. *Massachusetts Soldiers, Sailors, and Marines in the Civil War.* 9 vols. Norwood, Mass. 1932.

Maurice, Frederick, ed. *An Aide-De-Camp of Lee: Being the Papers of Colonel Charles Marshall Sometimes Aide-De-Camp,*

Military Secretary, and Assistant Adjutant General on the Staff of Robert E. Lee 1862–1865. Boston: Little, Brown, and Company, 1927.

McGee, B. F. *History of the 72nd Indiana Volunteer Infantry of the Mounted Lightning Brigade.* Ed. William R. Jewell. LaFayette, Ind.: S. Vater & Co., 1882.

McGuire, Hunter. *The Confederate Cause and Conduct in the War Between the States.* Richmond: L. H. Jenkins, 1907.

Moore, Frank, ed. *The Rebellion Record: A Diary of American Events.* 12 vols. New York: G. P. Putnam, 1862.

———. *The Civil War in Song and Story 1860–1865.* New York: P. F. Collier, 1889.

Morgan, James. *Abraham Lincoln, the Boy and the Man.* New York: Grosset & Dunlap, 1910.

Morris, Charles. *Half Hours with American History.* 2 vols. Philadelphia: J. B. Lippincott Company, 1887.

Mulholland, St. Clair A. *The Story of the 116th Regiment Pennsylvania Volunteers in the War of the Rebellion.* Philadelphia: F. McManus, Jr. & Co., 1903.

Pember, Phoebe Yates. *A Southern Woman's Story.* New York: G. W. Carleton & Co., 1879.

Rauscher, Frank. *Music on the March 1862–65 with the Army of the Potomac.* Philadelphia: William F. Fell & Co., 1892.

Raymond, Henry J. *The Life and Public Services of Abraham Lincoln.* New York: Derby and Miller Publishers, 1865.

Regimental Committee. *History of the One Hundred Twenty-fifth Regiment Pennsylvania Volunteers 1862–1863.* Philadelphia: J. B. Lippincott Company, 1906.

Rhodes, Robert Hunt, ed. *All for the Union: The Civil War Diary and Letters of Elisha Hunt Rhodes.* New York: Orion Books, 1985.

Roe, Alfred S. *The Tenth Regiment Massachusetts Volunteer Infantry 1861–1864.* Springfield, Mass: Tenth Regiment Veterans Assoc., 1909.

Sizer, Nelson and H. S. Drayton. *Heads and Faces and How to Study Them, A Manual of Phrenology and Physiognomy.* New York: Fowler & Wells Co., 1889.

Smith, Abram P. *History of the Seventy-Sixth Regiment New York Vol.* Cortland, N.Y.: Truair, Smith, and Miles, 1867.

Smith, W. B. *On Wheels and How I Came There.* New York: Hunt & Eaton, 1893.

Stackpole, Edward J. *Sheridan in the Shenandoah.* Harrisburg: Stackpole Books, 1992.

Stewart, Rev. Nixon B. *Dan McCook's Regiment 52nd O.V.I., A History of the Regiment, Its Campaigns and Battles from 1862 to 1865.* Published by the author, 1900.

Stimmel, Smith. *Personal Reminiscences of Abraham Lincoln.* Ed. LeRoy A. Fladseth. Kearney, Neb.: Morris Publishing, 1997.

Swisher, James K. *Prince of Edisto, Brigadier General Micah Jenkins C.S.A.* Berryville: Rockbridge Publishing Company, 1996.

Time Life Books, William C. Davis, ed. 27 vols. *Death in the Trenches: Grant at Petersburg,* Alexandria, Va.: Time-Life Books, 1986.

Trudeau, Noah Andrea. *The Last Citadel: Petersburg, Virginia June 1864-April 1865.* Boston: Little Brown & Company, 1991.

United States Capitol Historical Society. *We, the People: The Story of the United States Capitol.* Washington, D.C., 1976.

United States War Department. *A Compilation of the Official Records of the Union and Confederate Armies.* 128 vols. Washington, D.C., 1880–91.

Urban, John W. *My Experiences Mid Shot and Shell and in Rebel Den.* Lancaster: Published for the Author, 1892.

Utley, Robert Marshall. *Cavalier in Buckskin: George Armstrong Custer and the Western Military Frontier.* Norman: University of Oklahoma Press, 1988.

Warner, Ezra J. *Generals in Gray, Lives of the Confederate Commanders.* New Orleans: Louisiana State University Press, 1959.

———. *Generals in Blue, Lives of the Union Commanders.* New Orleans: Louisiana State University Press, 1964.

Washburn, George H. *A Complete Military History and Record of the 108th Regiment N.Y. Vols. From 1862 to 1894.* Rochester: E. R. Andrews, 1894.

Wert, Jeffery D. *From Winchester to Cedar Creek, The Shenandoah Campaign of 1864.* New York: Simon and Schuster, 1987.

Wilkeson, Frank. *Recollections of a Private Soldier in the Army of the Potomac.* London: George Redman, 1898.

Periodicals

America's Civil War, May 2000.

American Journal of Science and Arts. Vol. 82. November 1861.

Civil War Times Illustrated, January 1986.

Harper's Monthly Magazine, July 1865.

Harper's Weekly, July 1864.

The Lycoming Gazette, April 24, 1861.

Mifflinburg Telegraph, November 16, 1894.

The Milwaukee Telegraph, July 27, 1895.

New York Herald, April 16, 1861.

New York Times, July 4, 1861.

Philadelphia Daily Evening Bulletin, July 2, 1861.

Other

Lincoln, Abraham, Second Inaugural Address, March 4, 1865

National Archives and Records Administration

Index

– The Author –

Michael Sanders was born in Mifflinburg, Pennsylvania, and earned an associate's degree in agribusiness from Williamsport Area Community College. He graduated from Bloomsburg University of Pennsylvania and is currently teaching geography and American history at West Snyder Middle School in Beaver Springs, Pennsylvania. In addition, he owns and operates a farm near Mifflinburg with his wife, Bronwen, and son Owen.

CPSIA information can be obtained at www.ICGtesting.com
Printed in the USA
BVOW04s1437100514

353084BV00005B/16/P